Praise for

Stephanie Elg has a refreshingly open and positive approach on how to deal with depression and anxiety as a member of The Church of Jesus Christ of Latter-day Saints. Not only does she offer her own vulnerable experiences that most who have suffered with anxiety and depression can relate to, but she offers clinically relevant and practical ways of responding to these emotions while seeking a greater closeness to the Spirit. I believe the approach she describes in this book is inspired insight. Her humor, candidness, and intelligence will grasp the attention of any reader!

—Jonathan Harrop, Licensed Marriage and Family Therapist (LMFT) and Approved Supervisor for the American Association for Marriage and Family Therapists

Stephanie Elg shares with us her experiences discovering her own anxiety and depression and accepting her challenges for what they are. She explains how the adversary attempts to use our illnesses to keep us from feeling the love of God. She testifies to us that God never leaves us alone during trying times. This book is a must-read for those who want to accept and then find power over their anxiety and depression. She has masterfully shown us how to keep hope when we do not feel "Yellow."

—Matthew Wellock, MD

SEARCHING
FOR *Yellow*

SEARCHING FOR *Yellow*

Navigating
Depression & Anxiety
as a Latter-day Saint

STEPHANIE ELG

Copyright © 2022 by Stephanie Elg

All rights reserved, including the right to reproduce this book, or portions thereof, in any form. No part of this book may be used or reproduced in any manner whatsoever without written permission from the publisher, except in the case of brief quotations embodied in critical articles and reviews. The views expressed herein are the responsibility of the author and do not necessarily represent the position of the publisher. For information or permission, visit her website, stephanieelg.com.

This is a work of creative nonfiction. The events herein are portrayed to the best of the author's memory. While all the stories in this book are true, some names and identifying details may have been changed to protect the privacy of the people involved.

This material is neither made, provided, approved, nor endorsed by Intellectual Reserve, Inc. or The Church of Jesus Christ of Latter-day Saints. Any content or opinions expressed, implied or included in or with the material are solely those of the owner and not those of Intellectual Reserve, Inc. or The Church of Jesus Christ of Latter-day Saints.

The author of this book does not dispense medical advice or prescribe the use of any technique as a form of treatment for physical, emotional, or medical problems without the advice of a physician, either directly or indirectly. The intent of the author is only to offer information of a general nature to help you in your quest for health and well-being. In the event you use any of the information in this book for yourself, the author assumes no responsibility for your actions.

Photo credit: Meredith Evans
Cover design by MiblArt
Illustrations by Tom Tolman
Interior print design and layout by Marny K. Parkin
Ebook design and layout by Marny K. Parkin

CB

Published by Covered Bridges Publishing, LLC

979-8-218-00719-5

To my husband, Darren, and my kids and grandkids,
Alison, Brad, Natalie, Austin, Kate, Hudson, Brixly, Leo,
and to all those who will join our family. Here's to us having a
blast while we serve, help, and love others along the way.

Contents

Action

Preface

Why in the World Write About Something So Depressing?

THOUGH FOR YEARS the Lord prodded me to write, I refused. Well, I skirted around it at first, toying with fictional novels and other stuff, but I refused to go "there." Finally, after some strong but gentle chastising from Him, I conceded. Okay, fine. I would write what I knew, bury it under my mattress, and my kids could read it after I died. For reals. There was no reason to expose my rawest, darkest moments to *anyone*. It's . . . well . . . it's depressing. It's horrible. And there's more: once you toss it out to the world, you can't take it back. You're hosed.

I could tell the Lord was satisfied with the compromise I'd presented, so I began to write. I wrote about what I was experiencing and feeling. I recorded the anger, the loneliness, the pain.

After a year or two, and much to my delight, I realized that some of what I was writing could be put into a spreadsheet. I love spreadsheets! It's so much easier for my brain to wrap around something in a spreadsheet.

As I looked at the spreadsheets, my experiences began to take shape. I was able to see the missing pieces, but I didn't know what to fill them in with. After all, I'd worked hard to forget each episode of depression or anxiety, leaving me with little memory to which I could refer.

Soon, an unexpected thing began to happen. As I wrote during my bouts of depression or anxiety, I was finally able to fill in the gaps in my spreadsheet and add to or tweak those already in place. In a strange sort of way, it gave me a sense of accomplishment even in the middle of my private nightmare.

And the more I wrote, the more I realized how shocked my family would be to find a manuscript under my mattress someday. I had tried to hide my pain and agony from them in order to create a healthy, happy life for all of us, but I slowly began to recognize there were lessons in life I didn't want to wait to share. I wanted others to see the Lord's hand in their lives as it had been in mine.

Fine. I agreed to write it, and I even agreed to print it, but there's *no way* I was going to put my name on it. No, sir. I would need a really cool pen name.

My maiden name is Friend, which is pretty awesome, so I could have gone with that. But there would still be people who knew me, so that wouldn't work. My current last name, Elg, means "moose" in Swedish. There you go. I went from being a Friend to a Moose. Could my alias be Stephanie Moose? Lame. I knew had to set aside the nightmare of coming up with a cool alias name and just stick to the writing. With that, I at least felt like I was getting somewhere. So I wrote.

And as I read what I had written over the years, I was shocked. My experiences had become reality. As I'd pushed my experiences aside over time, I'd regularly wondered if I was exaggerating how I felt or simply not emotionally tough enough to deal with a bad day. I read my notes and shuddered as I remembered moments I wanted to forget.

Then a funny thing happened. I actually began to feel more confident with what I was experiencing. Being able to refer to my writings solidified what I knew deep down: The pain is yucky, raw, and real. But I recognized there were ups and downs, and I was able to accept myself more. I felt braver and began to share thoughts, emotions, and experiences with loved ones. I was able to see the Lord's hand not only in pulling me out of the dark but *during* times of darkness.

As I shared more of my journey with friends and family, I realized how much shame I had held on to over the years. Honestly, I don't particularly like the phrase "Don't be ashamed." It sounds like I should be arrogant or something, like I have to stick my chest out and be in people's faces about my depression and anxiety issues. Regardless, it is shame that prevents us from openly discussing mental health.

After decades of writing, the Lord let me know it was time—time to remove the shame, compile what I had written, and put *my name* on it. I can tell you it hasn't been easy. Satan has fought me hard and torn my self-worth apart. But with this book, I push forward, and Heavenly Father continues to help me conquer my fears while I show others how I continue to search for yellow.

Interpreting Yellow

Chapter 1

The Consistent Winner

Demanding Relief from the Pain of Depression and Anxiety

IF I WERE to ask what your favorite color is, what would you say? Blue? Orange? Pink? What color speaks to you? Maybe you can't pick a favorite. Maybe you like all of them.

As for me? I *cannot* commit. I just can't do it! Oh, I've tried. When I finally decide on a favorite color, I get bored with it within two days. I'm ready to move on to the next color that catches my eye. Sometimes it's that light blue-green mix. I don't even know what it's called. The next day I'm off to white. Just plain ol' clean, calming white.

Purple!

My sister-in-law's favorite color is purple. Lisa wears purple clothes. Purple jewelry. She even decorates her house in purple. Well, at least as much as her husband will allow. It sure makes it easy to buy her a gift. Get her any ol' color shirt, and she's a sweetie, so grateful and kind. Give her something purple, and she's over the moon! "Oh, I *love* it! Thank you! It's my favorite color!" As if none of us knew. Bam. Job well done.

My kids often demand to know my favorite color. I'm not sure why, but, evidently, it's an important thing for them to know. I can't just say, "I don't have a favorite color." I have to declare my favorite right then and there. So what do I say when I must choose a single color that defines me?

Yellow. It's my go-to. Not because I want all my walls painted yellow or all my outfits to be yellow. Okay, so my kitchen table *did* use to be a bright mustard yellow—but no judging. I just like yellow. Maybe it's because it best represents what I want in life.

Mustard Yellow

If I had my way, yellow would wake me up in the mornings and tuck me in at night. It would manage all my moments and experiences. Yellow is calming, joyful, and sunshine-y. Yellow describes who I want to be, what I want to become, and what I hope to experience. I want to be a yellow person—not only to others but deep inside my soul. The more yummy, happy, comforting yellow experiences I can have, the better.

Unfortunately, nobody experiences yellow all the time. I know I don't. In fact, more often than not, yellow has felt unattainable to me. For decades, I've had bouts of panic, depression, and suicidal thoughts. Years ago, I was diagnosed with depression and anxiety. The diagnosis was maddening, and I hoped to turn things around quickly. I wanted this nasty battle to simply disappear. The faster, the better.

Years later, I've figured out that my struggle with depression and anxiety may not be over in mortality. Instead, it looks as if these two challenges were handpicked to be some of my monstrous earthly trials. And while these are the cards I have been dealt, I refuse to allow them to stop me from experiencing the relief and power of yellow.

So, how do I tackle this big ol' undertaking?

At first, I couldn't even figure out what I was searching for. I simply knew I needed relief. But as I paid attention, I began to notice patterns and techniques, some of which helped, some of which hurt. For example, pushing myself to accomplish small goals was helpful, but too many high expectations proved detrimental. Having a better understanding of positive and negative patterns and techniques has helped me not only understand myself but resulted in greater opportunities to experience the yellow I so intensely desired.

Finding ways to lessen the pain has been empowering and utterly exciting. I want to share them with you in the hope that we may be able to search for and feel yellow together. Though we may not be able to experience yellow every day, it can pop into and out of our lives a lot. As a matter of fact, we should expect it. Demand it.

Side by side, we can push past the struggle and replace it with the yellow that keeps us hopeful, alive, and looking forward to the next day. Let's do this. Together.

Chapter 2

Yummmmmm

What Exactly Are We Searching For?

IF I HAD to describe yellow in one word, it would be *yummy*. Yellow is the feeling we have during our yummy moments and experiences. It includes peace, happiness, warmth, love, goodness, reassurance, and hope.

While we experience yellow when feeling God's love and Spirit, powerful spiritual experiences aren't the only times we feel yellow. Yellow includes tiny flecks of aha!

Yellow is an adventure with God. It is recognizing His hand in everyday moments. **Searching for yellow is the act of striving to find the Spirit in our lives no matter what stage of suffering we may be in.** It is awareness of the good and the blessings around us. It is inklings of insight into His plan. Yellow is rejuvenating and gives us comfort and hope. It's the joy of knowing God is by our side.

All of us have dark moments behind closed doors, but yellow lets us believe there are better moments ahead. Don't get me wrong: searching for yellow is not simply "looking at the bright side and getting over it." This is *not* the case.

Yellow is much more than that. It includes a wide array of experiences and feelings. It can last for a split second or for hours. (Sheesh! Wouldn't it be awesome if it always lasted for hours?) Let's get real: our yellow varies from moment to moment, day to day.

Yellow surprises and amazes. It can be fun and spontaneous. Some yellows linger, while other yellows unpredictably pop in and out of our lives.

———

Here's the great part: the more we search for yellow, the more it appears. The beauty of yellow is that it's not restricted. It's a gift from God, and He wants us to have as much yellow as possible.

Here's another great thing: Those suffering from depression and anxiety can still experience yellow. God promises to be with us, but depression and anxiety can prevent us from feeling Him near. Even though we may not always be able to feel His Spirit, the act of searching for yellow is **choosing** to keep Him close. It's choosing to watch for Him in our lives. When we conscientiously search for yellow, we willingly stand by Him.

When we search for yellow, we're telling God that despite our circumstances, we will continue to look for Him and ask to feel His Spirit. Searching for yellow assures us that once the depression and anxiety lift, we are ready and willing to feel His love and Spirit once again.

When we search for yellow, what is it we are searching for?

- Spiritual moments
- Peace/comfort

- Calm
- Reassurance
- Feelings of confidence with the Lord
- Moments/glimpses of relief
- Feelings of hope
- Believing there is hope
- Looking for God in our lives in different and simple ways

Chapter 3

And It Hits

Clues Given from Our Mind and Body

IT'S A FAMILIAR feeling, but I despise it. Maybe you can relate. An invisible weight seems to crush my body. It's as if the air around me has become dense and oppressive. Even small tasks, like getting out of bed, getting dressed, and smiling at my children, have become insurmountably difficult. I have to fight each task and feel like throwing up. Why? For crying out loud, WHY?!

I feel completely stupid. If I were just this or that, things would be different. If I were just emotionally and physically tougher. More righteous. Instead, my weaknesses show up all at once. They are evil little devils that haunt me, follow me wherever I go. They *especially* love to attack me when I'm down. Their voices scream in my head and consume my thoughts. Their presence adds to the weight in the air around me. Right now, the devils are winning. I give up. They are right. I will never be good enough, strong enough.

Right away, right this minute, my life feels unbearable. I plead for the darkness to be taken away, but it continues to

haunt me. The devils start to laugh in my
face. At my weaknesses. At my insecurities. At my imperfections.

STOP!

I have to stop. It's time. The darkness is too familiar. Too thick. I recognize it, and I want the darkness to
lift. I want those little devils to leave me
alone and let me breathe. I have to decide. I
must call it what it is. I have to be honest with
where I am emotionally. It's the only way.

But I also must remember where I want to be. That's more
important. I want to see yellow again. I want to *feel* yellow
again. It doesn't even have to last long. Just *something*.

———

When depression and anxiety first hit, before we become familiar with them, we may not know exactly what's happening. The
darkness and confusion can strike quickly and unexpectedly.
We might notice something is "off," but we may not be able to
pinpoint what's wrong.

I've found it helpful to read the "clues" in my reactions.
Some of the things that immediately clue me in when I'm experiencing depression are: My thoughts get dark, and it's difficult
for me to physically move. In regards to anxiety, I not only
notice difficulty breathing and my heart racing, I also notice
how much effort it takes to focus on the simplest of things.

The more we begin to notice, the greater chance we have of
improving our current situation. Our mind and body can help
us understand the degree of depression and/or anxiety we may
be experiencing.

Mind

· Difficulty focusing/remembering

· Difficulty making decisions

· Sadness/hopelessness

· Questioning whether things will get better

· Inability to relax or stop worrying

· Feeling you are a failure or constantly letting others down

· Wishing you were not alive

· Feeling as if you live in fear

· Avoiding things that would trigger anxiety

Body

· Lacking energy or motivation/extremely tired

· Finding it hard to fall asleep or stay asleep

· Waking up feeling anxious in the middle of the night

· Feeling nervous or restless/trembling

· Sweating

· Racing heartbeat/chest pains

· Tight muscles

· Rapid breathing

· Changes in appetite/nausea

· Dizziness

· Avoiding being around other people

That's a long list. It's no wonder depression and anxiety can completely consume our lives. We can get even more understanding about the degree of depression and anxiety we may be experiencing by asking ourselves these questions:

- Do I constantly feel negative or gloomy?
- Do I feel no emotion (numb)?
- Do I frequently feel fear?
- Do I feel as if my thoughts are overpowering and controlling me?
- Do I wake up in a panic in the middle of the night?
- Have I lost motivation?
- Am I reacting sharply to those around me?
- Am I having a difficult time feeling the Spirit?
- Am I physically/emotionally safe?
- Am I having thoughts of harming myself or committing suicide?
- What specific things in my life have been affected? (These could be things like sleep or the ability to communicate with others.)

It can be crushing to face this reality. For years, I simply denied my problems. It was embarrassing to admit there was an issue. But it was just as embarrassing—if not even more so—to have my loved ones see me struggle repeatedly.

The battle seemed too great to tackle. I had lots of questions. *What is happening? Where do I begin? Why me?* But I knew I wanted something different, which meant I also knew something needed to change. That's when I started pushing for yellow. And every time I felt just a few glimpses of yellow, I also felt a refreshing lift from the heavy weight of darkness.

Chapter 4

New Dreams Work Too

Attacking the Cycles of Depression and Anxiety

I'm just waking up. My body feels shaky. My heart is racing, and my breathing is shallow. I feel weak, but the thought of food turns my stomach. If I move too quickly, I get even dizzier, and my vision blacks out. My mind is unnecessarily alert, and my senses are heightened; everything is louder and more exaggerated. I feel unsafe and am filled with fear, even though I can't identify any immediate danger.

I need to find the energy to fight the physical weakness. I must get food so my predicament doesn't worsen and become a panic attack. Even though that makes me feel sicker, I force myself to eat.

The darkness *will not win*. Today I can push through it, keep moving. It takes much longer than it should to complete simple tasks, but I don't let that stop me. I have started searching for yellow.

I pray, pleading to feel some relief. Nothing happens. My mind feels hollow and jumbled all at the same time. I turn on calming music. Nope. That doesn't help. I switch to invigorating music and decide that may work.

I continue to pray, asking the Lord what I can do to find yellow. Nothing comes to mind, so I continue getting ready for the day. I'm still not sure what's causing all this. Does Satan want to keep me from having a good day? Or is all this just me? I decide to blame Satan. The music starts to speak to me and helps me relax. I can breathe just a bit now. Time to turn it up and absorb some yellow.

The more I accomplish, even if it's just small stuff, the more emotionally and physically strong I become. I choose to wear my sunshine shirt since it has some yellow on it. I vow to buy more clothes with yellow as a symbolic reminder. The day has started, and I am determined to make the most of it.

———

I never want anyone to see me at my most vulnerable. It's so deeply personal and raw. It's so much easier to simply avoid people. Eliminates the risk.

Each day is difficult enough—but when the darkest days hit, it feels completely hopeless. I try to drown myself in my covers when I'm haunted by hellish emotional darkness. Shaking and sobbing in my closet, I wish the floor would swallow me whole. I've worked hard to keep from revealing this grueling emotional pain to anyone. I want to be, to feel, to experience normal. But I don't even know what normal is.

I used to dream of a life without depression and anxiety. I don't dream that anymore. I know—that sounds horribly pessimistic, but bear with me for a sec. It has actually helped me to accept it.

Here's what used to happen: I would drop emotionally, bulldoze through my struggles, and become understandably excited when they were over. I was relieved to think I would never have to suffer like that again. I would pick myself up and move on with life as if nothing had happened, refusing to look back.

That worked until the pendulum swung back and I found myself feeling more discouraged than before. Denying the repetitive nature of my depression and anxiety wasn't doing me any good. I cycled the same cycle. I fought the same battle without new strategies or game plans. Walls that should have been torn down stood firm and, worse yet, in the way of progression. I seemed to be continually proving I was a failure.

I'm honestly not sure when I started to admit that this would be a lifetime ordeal. For years, I hoped and prayed that with time, my depression and anxiety would go away. Some people suffer from depression and anxiety because of their circumstances, while others are genetically disposed to it. Sometimes it's both. But no matter what causes depression and anxiety, it's a cruel experience.

I didn't believe that simply pushing away depression and anxiety as needed was a bad plan. It meant survival. But then I started to wonder. I realized I was stuck in a vicious cycle, and

I saw how it affected me and those around me. And I didn't like what I saw. I wanted something different. I wanted better. And that's when things started to change.

I began to search for help. I went to psychologists and psychiatrists, but none of them clicked. I tried various medications. Some worked better than others. It was miserable. I guess I expected a quick fix; instead, it was a long, drawn-out process filled with hurdles and stumbling blocks.

Still, I wanted yellow. The urge for it became even more intense. I wondered how I could get it more often.

I began to pay attention. To everything—to my surroundings, the way I spoke, the way I reacted. I began noting the things that triggered or calmed me. And as I watched, I learned. Without realizing it, I had officially started my own remodeling process. I had officially started searching for yellow.

———

And here's the best part: as we persevere and keep pushing for our own yellow, we find things from our past experiences that increase our understanding. Through a great deal of patience, we can find doctors and therapists who'll pay attention to our specific needs. We learn to tweak our thoughts and the ways we react, and we become more aware of ourselves.

Unfortunately, the new awareness doesn't mean it's all over. As I continue to cycle through periods of depression and anxiety, I am frustrated again and again. The debris from these episodes lingers even after I get through the tough experiences. As I am plunged into another episode, I beg for the depression and anxiety to simply end.

My situation continues to be incredibly difficult. It pains me to say that I still have severe drops in mood and panic attacks. I still have moments, days, and even months when I can't function. I wish I could tell you it all goes away. So far, it hasn't.

But there's a big difference now: I have more yellow than ever before. The drops are less frequent. The moments, days, and months are better. I can assess where I am emotionally and better regulate the episodes of depression and anxiety when they do come. And get this—I am actually able to have hope while *in* the depths of my darkest moments. Okay. I may not *feel* hope at the time, but I *know* it. I have seen the yellow, and I know it will be back.

Chapter 5

The Personal Adventure

The Four Phases We Need to Succeed

MIND. BODY. THOUGHTS. Feelings. Movements. Reactions. Words. The emotional assault seems all-consuming. The never-ending-ness of this beast is draining. Avoiding the inevitable darkness is impossible, so what choice do we have? It feels hopeless.

Ironically, we hide from the world, then are baffled as to how we can fight such a battle alone. We plead for relief, knowing we want to escape from the agony but not knowing how that will ever happen. We're not convinced we have the strength, the fortitude, the will. We just want out. Grasping at straws, we look for solutions but are wary about trying something new. The possibility of additional decline is terrifying. To be put in such a vulnerable place feels cruel.

But then we realize—it's not what we want, but it's what we have been given. It's time to pursue what we *do* want. We want different. We want better. It's time for us to discover the meaning of yellow and how to get it in our lives. It's time to make a change. It's go time!

———

Sifting through who we are, what we have experienced, and what we are currently experiencing creates a combat zone that's exclusive to us—a battle like none other. We need to fight for yellow in a way that's unique and individual.

Even though our fight is unique, the path to yellow includes four basic phases. It's the four *A*s: **Awareness, Acceptance, Assessment, and Action.**

Awareness. Developing an awareness of our current emotional state gives us the opportunity to explore what we have been experiencing as well as what we *want* to experience. Being mindful of our current and past emotional adventures—whether good or bad—opens the door to progress. Without knowing this, we're asking for emotional reruns.

Acceptance. We need to admit to ourselves that depression and anxiety are simply part of our personal earthly struggles. We need to take ownership and assume responsibility for the things we have done and continue to do. As we accept our situation, we not only acknowledge the control depression and anxiety seem to have in our lives, but we declare that we are willing to fight the battle, even when it looks like it may never end.

Assessment. Once we accept our struggles, it's time to assess where we are and where we would like to be. We begin inspecting previous and current experiences and how we've been affected by them. We watch for triggers and obstacles that prevent or hinder us from moving forward. We determine what changes we need to make to reach our new goals. This might seem intimidating at first, but we do it one chunk at a time. Each new insight signifies progress.

Action. Quickly, it becomes time to act—to do something about what we have learned. As we act, we become actively engaged in changing our environments, attitudes, and decisions. We watch for and relish each yellow moment. And whatever happens, we mustn't overlook inviting the Spirit into our lives. Seeking the Spirit lets the Lord know we are serious about not only finding yellow but staying by His side as we move forward despite darkness or being unable to feel Him near.

AWARENESS
CCEPTANCE
SSESSMENT
CTION

A word of caution: It's important not to get stuck between these phases. Though we should always allow ourselves time to regroup, we should be aware of the danger of not moving forward. For example, we may be tempted to become bitter or refuse responsibility after the acceptance or assessment phases. We could also become angry after the action phase if we experience no immediate change or any yellow. Remember, the Lord works in His own due time. As we are patient with Him and what He wants us to learn, we open opportunities for beautiful changes to occur.

Awareness

Being Mindful of
What We Are Experiencing

Chapter 6

Ups and Downs

Learning to Use an Awareness Arc

IT WAS CHRISTMAS morning, and we were excited to go snowmobiling as a family. Since we lived in Arizona, this would be an experience we would never forget.

Getting the forty-five thousand layers of clothing on was educational. We then anxiously shuffled outside to start riding.

We learned a few things about snowmobiling throughout the day. First of all, don't let anyone tell you that you can simply pack food and eat it on the trail. Nope. It's not that

simple. My son preferred to starve himself rather than unearth all the layers of clothing from his face and hands to get a pb&j out of his backpack. The cold is . . . well . . . like death.

Even though we almost froze our faces off, we continued to ride our hearts out. The day ended up being full of emotional and physical ups and downs. At one point, I started having a panic attack on the trail. (I just love how those obnoxious episodes like to show up unannounced.) No worries, though; I was able to pull through it and get back to riding. We even got lost a few times, and our snowmobiles kept running off the trail and slamming into snowbanks. (We later found out that's normal and no big deal. Who knew?) Oh, and did I mention it was *cold*?

After riding for the greater part of the day, we reached the top of the mountain. The beauty of the snow-capped trees lit-

erally took my breath away. It was a moment I caught on camera, but more importantly, I wanted to catch it in my heart. The photos did the beauty complete injustice. Few times in my life have I ever seen something so strikingly stunning. I mentally captured the moment of yellow and quickly continued on the trail alongside the rest of my family. I replayed the images as I added new ones on the way. Just for a moment, nothing seemed like it could take away from that heavenly experience.

That's where things went wrong. What seemed like only a handful of minutes later, I pulled up to a cluster of my family, their snowmobiles at a standstill. There had been an accident, and it was my kid.

My daughter had lost control of her snowmobile while going . . . well, faster than she should have. She flew off her machine, blacked out, and woke up on the snow-covered gravel. She quickly stood but was very wobbly. As I pulled up and began assessing the situation, she passed out.

Immediately after she woke up again, we realized we were running low on gas and were lost somewhere on the wrong side of the mountain. Bad news. As we stood on the trail, the sun started sinking below the horizon. We had heard the nighttime temp was going to be minus five—a bit cold for us winter-weather-wimpy Arizonans. Genuine fear quickly set in, and we started to pray.

Within about three minutes, a miracle happened. Two men pulled up on snowmobiles. One of them "just so happened to be" a fireman and paramedic. Oh, and he used to work for search and rescue on the mountain. Go figure. He assessed the situation and evaluated my daughter. He calmed our nerves and showed us where to park our snowmobiles overnight. He and his friend then drove more than an hour out of their way to drop us off at our car. Refusing any sort of payment, the strangers slipped away onto the snow-filled roads, seemingly naive to the miracle they had been in our lives.

Christmas that year was not what we expected. It was much more emotionally and physi-cally grueling than we could have imagined. That evening, we sat by the fire drinking hot chocolate and trying to relax as we reflected on the traumatizing events of the day and counted our blessings: we were together and alive.

———

Though her concussion was severe, my daughter was lucky her injuries were not more serious. The doctors told us she was lucky to be alive. Although it was a physically and emotionally long and painful process, she has since fully recovered.

Reliving that day is not on my to-do list. Let's chalk it up as done. Don't wanna go back. The negative moments were overwhelming and, honestly, terrifying. Even so, we have been so grateful as we've taken a closer look at the miracles of that day.

Our lives are a journey full of these ups and downs. We may hit obstacles and at times completely fall off the sled and then have to get up and check for bruises and damage. The fall is all we remember until we take a second glance. Then we realize our days have also included snow-capped trees and yellow moments. We find that Heavenly Father is beside us even as we fall and that He provides each of us (sometimes not-so-obvious) miracles.

———

We'd all like to be in total control of our lives, but we know that's not possible. No matter how much we plan and prepare, we can never guarantee a perfect outcome. At some point, we will have a greater understanding of our trials. Meanwhile, the Lord wants us to learn and grow along the way.

Dealing with depression and anxiety can bring ups and downs to our daily lives. During some of the downs, we might feel bruised, damaged, and lucky to have survived. It might not be possible to fully control our depression and anxiety, but through personal awareness, we can lay a foundation for stronger emotional balance. We can get great insight by taking a close look at how we are doing generally.

Similar to the ups and downs of the snowmobile trail, we experience fluid ups and downs with our depression and anxiety. Take a moment to envision an arc that describes your current depression or anxiety. Consider how you've been feeling the past few days, weeks, or even months. There may be great fluctuation in your arc or seemingly none at all.

This graph is an example of what my arc might look like on any given day. I assess depression and anxiety separately as I deal with them. Sometimes I experience them consecutively. Other times, they are separate.

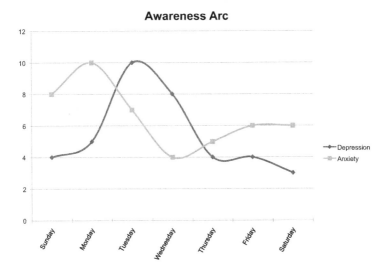

What does your arc(s) look like? You may find it helpful to get into the habit of doing regular awareness checks on your arc/s. As we observe our emotions and reactions, we may recognize triggers we haven't noticed. We can create personal awareness and connect reactions to experiences. This allows us to pinpoint where we stand emotionally. We can determine if our arc seems to be going in a positive direction, how fast it moves, or how quickly it fluctuates. The more we pay attention, the easier it becomes. Being aware means looking back so we can determine how to move forward.

Chapter 7

The Taste Test

The More We Experiment,
the Greater the Opportunity for Relief

IT ALL STARTED with a simple apple taste test.

Decades ago, my mom brought home a variety of apples from the grocery store. She cut them into slices, and each of us kids was to figure out which was our favorite. Little did she know what an obsession she created! All these years later, taste testing has become one of my family's favorite things to do. Obviously, our taste testing comes from the sugar aisle rather than the fruits or veggies, but, hey!

Here's how we do it. First, we assemble plates and forks, along with water to cleanse the palate as needed. Next, we break out the spreadsheet. Yup, you heard me right. This is serious business, people. Finally, we break out the buckets of ice cream or slices of pie and meticulously taste the flavors one at a time; each of us gives each selection a score between one and ten. We go through each variety comparing, critiquing, and having a sugar-high blast!

Recently, we tasted cookies. We bought a huge variety of different flavors from a specialty cookie shop in the area. They have your typical flavors, like chocolate chip and sugar, but also dozens of specialty flavors. I was pleasantly surprised with their Raspberry Lemonade cookie. It was a slam dunk! I was anxious to keep trying my luck with the Frozen Hot Chocolate cookie, but I was gravely disappointed. Boo on the Frozen Hot Chocolate cookie.

Each taste test ends with a few surprises. We think we automatically know our favorites, but we can't always be sure. Each willingly dives in to try all options. We listen to others' assessments and laugh at the commentary. We learn about ourselves as well as about each other.

As I have paid painstaking attention to the way I react to things during each phase of depression and anxiety, I have learned a great deal about myself. I have learned what helps and what doesn't help when searching for my yellow. I have found that what pushes me toward yellow one moment or day may not work the next day. This was frustrating until I recognized that, at least for me, this was normal. Let's get real, though. Assessing where we are emotionally is not quite like tasting a plate of cookies. I get it. But it can be a similar process.

How? Well, first, we must be willing to try. It is essential for us to be game on. This does not mean we are mechanically plowing full speed ahead. Rather, we must be willing to lean in and experiment a bit. Think about taste-testing; we aren't taking massive bites of each thing. It's small, slow, and steady.

In our attempt to find yellow, we will discover that some things work for us and some don't. What I do to find yellow may be completely different from what you do, and that's okay. Nobody says we have to have the same journey or experiences. The trick is that the more we try, the greater the chance is that we will find yellow.

———

Searching for and finding yellow are two separate things. *Searching* is the process. It's the looking, the trying, the pushing. It's putting the cookie on our plate and tasting it, perhaps comparing it to others we've tasted. *Finding* yellow is the actual encounter with goodness. It's the joy of the new flavor that catches us off guard. It's feeling the Spirit and discovering brief instances— or longer periods if we're lucky—of reprieve and hope.

Compiling and tweaking your list of what to do when searching for yellow is a continual process. Just remember that new cookie flavors are brought on the market all the time. Yesssssssssss! We all have our go-to flavors, but as new ones are presented and we try them out, we may find our list of things that "taste good," or work for us, expanding.

As our list develops, we must keep in mind that the items on that list may not help every time. I may find myself going through the whole list and finding only one thing—or maybe nothing at all—that helps right then. Don't give up! It can be frustrating at first, but remember that with everything you do to search for yellow, you are moving in the right direction. You are inviting the Lord into your life by actively doing the things that bring peace, comfort, and hope. That means you are making progress!

~ Things I Do to *Search* for My Yellow ~

At Home

- Wood projects
- Refurbishing projects
- Rearrange a room
- Bake bread
- Cook on my own or with my family
- Take time to laugh
- Allow myself to cry and release built-up emotions
- Breathe slowly and deeply
- Paint
- Take a nap
- Do the dishes
- Place a cold washcloth/ice pack on my neck or forehead
- Take a shower
- Cuddle on the couch
- Enjoy the scent of candles, cookies, and bread
- Take helpful herbs or medications
- Tense and relax my muscles
- Get a massage
- Have a dance party with the family
- Read a novel

Out and About

- Spend time alone outside
- Serve someone else

- Go for a walk
- Go out for lunch
- Go for a bike ride
- Go for a drive with the window down

Visual

- Watch my loved ones smile
- Watch the sunrise/sunset
- Watch the trees blow in the wind
- Watch the rain/monsoons/lightning
- Watch an uplifting, calming, and/or funny show

Hearing

- Blast music
- Listen to quiet music
- Enjoy the silence
- Talk with friends
- Sing around the house with my family
- Listen to nature
- Visit with my therapist

Writing

- Write down thoughts
- List accomplishments for the day
- Write someone a note
- Create a list of things I am grateful for
- Make a to-do list and determine the priorities
- Write positive affirmations on the mirror

Touching the Heartstrings

- Stop in the moment and create a pause for my mind
- Pray alone or with my family
- Read my patriarchal blessing
- Listen to or read conference talks
- Read the scriptures
- Avoid comparing myself to others
- Surround myself with people who uplift me
- Forgive
- Achieve a goal
- Think positive thoughts about myself
- Give myself credit for trying
- Repeat positive thoughts (brain repetition)
- Reflect on past experiences that have brought me peace
- Remind myself there is hope for future yellow

Addressing Concerns

- Get off social media
- Limit TV, phone, and so on
- Avoid damaging thoughts
- Avoid damaging people and situations

It's time to get creative. Don't limit yourself to a few things as you search for your yellow. Depending on your situation and motivation level, use various techniques and opportunities to create your list. Push yourself while looking for and experimenting with things that bring you closer to the Lord, then allow time for the yellow to come.

Chapter 8

Don't Mess with Success

Relief Can Come from Unexpected Places

I RECENTLY BENT over and pulled out a weed. Trust me, it wasn't out of the goodness of my heart. It was because I was frustrated. I was sick of feeling such darkness, and I thought if I could rip the weed to shreds, I might feel some relief.

Actually, it did feel kinda good, so I pulled out another, then another. I yanked, twisted, and dug at the weeds, which felt so symbolic of my life. I wished I could get rid of my heaviness as quickly as I could each weed.

As my pile of weeds grew, I began to think and process. Working through my emotions allowed me to get to a calmer state. I began to ponder, sift, sort, and talk to God. Little did

I know it, but I was beginning to fight for yellow. I was opening a window to yellow. Without being aware, my search for
yellow had begun.

Then, unexpectedly, I felt it—a moment of clarity and calm,
a moment that told me that although things in my life hadn't
changed, it would be okay. I had found yellow. Who knew I
would find yellow while cleaning dirt from under my nails? But
I couldn't deny it; it was there. I relished the brief instant that
the yellow showed up, and I pled for it to stay.

As it so often does, the heaviness of my depression and anxiety quickly returned. But now I knew that if I continued my
search, yellow would sneak in and jolt me again. My job then
was to simply put the treasured moment in my pocket and tuck
it away for when I needed to savor it again.

To this day, I continue to try to find yellow by pulling weeds
and hosing off the porch. I'm convinced that when I'm doing
this, my husband actually thinks I'm being Mrs. Worker Bee,
but nope. Not really. I am processing. And if I can impress him
while processing, then, bonus!

———

Every bit of me begs to run away. I repeatedly think about
where I can drive or fly. Who can I go visit? I need an escape.
I dissect my calendar and realize it's no use. I'm feeling like
at the end of the trip, I will be in the same place as when I
started—with my demons still facing me. Running away from
my emotions will not resolve the issues.

I pretty much hate everything and everyone around me.
I know I'm in the wrong, but I don't care. Life is cruel and
unfair. I'm sick of feeling abandoned and useless. I have failed
at being a mom and wife. I've failed in my calling and as a

friend. I can do nothing productive or worthwhile. I have failed with God. I'm sick of these thoughts but can't escape them.

I decide to bake. It has helped before, and I can only hope it helps again. If anything, with fresh bread coming out of the oven, my kids will think I'm the bee's knees despite how dark I feel on the inside. I drag myself to the pantry. I decide on croissants.

I take off my rings and tie my apron. It's time to get serious, people. Though the milk, butter, and sugar should cause some excitement, I just feel like lying down and throwing up. My brain is in a fog, and I need to read and reread the instructions. My body is heavy and not wanting to make the croissants, but I stay committed.

As I continue, I begin to wonder how in the world people used to do it—making meals from scratch every day, I mean. Starting fires in order to cook rather than pushing a button on the oven. Being in a rut of depression but not having any quick-fix meals. No washing machines to keep up on the laundry. I can't imagine.

My mind begins to relax as I focus on the task at hand. The dough is warm to the touch, and its mild but sweet aroma begins to fill the kitchen. Rolling and cutting the dough into triangles is relaxing. I am aware my trials have not gone away, nor has my life changed, but I am filled with encouragement. For a moment, I feel yellow.

By the time the croissants are headed into the oven, a feeling of accomplishment has set in. A sense of calm fills my heart, and I am pleased with my efforts. I've pushed through the hard and made some progress. I've had a temporary reprieve. I anxiously wait for the timer to go off. When the kids get home from school, they will be so excited. I just know it.

Oftentimes we will find the relief in unexpected places, but we must not overlook that we may find yellow right in front of us.

My husband sees new people at work all the time. Sometimes he has lengthy chats with them; other times their encounters are short. He never knows what to expect, and because he is great at keeping information confidential, he doesn't share much about those conversations.

One day, though, he came home looking quite concerned. He mentioned he had been having a conversation with someone who gives others Botox injections to reduce their wrinkles. Within a few minutes of their brief conversation, she suggested she give him Botox for his crow's feet. He asked what I thought. I paused. I looked at him in confusion, then proceeded to examine his face. He does have crow's feet, but I had never thought of them as a problem. I thought about him getting Botox and instantly decided that was a fat *no*!

First of all, my husband is the most handsome man in the world, so why mess with perfection? Second, I happen to love those crow's feet. When I see his crow's feet, it means happiness and joy. It means he is laughing, smiling, or being silly around the house. His crow's feet are my yellow—so back off, woman!

Acceptance

Processing the Hand We Have Been Dealt

Chapter 9

Call It What It Is

Coming to Grips with Reality

THE REALITY THAT depression and anxiety seem to be a never-ending part of my life has been more than discouraging. For years, I didn't want to face it; I denied it. I visited multiple therapists and doctors, went on and off medications, and envisioned a quick fix. So as the depression and anxiety continued to cycle over and over, I was devastated.

I had desperately hoped it would simply go away, a temporary trial that simply faded into the past. But after years of ups and downs, I slowly began to realize that it was going to be a consistent part of my story. I hated that about myself. It made me feel angry and weak. Was this a punishment from God? If so, what had I done to deserve it? Did I really need to go through something so dark and difficult to be a better person? Maybe I was simply not strong enough to handle my trials.

As I have come to grips with my reality, I have decided to fight it. Believe me, there are plenty of times when I'm not sure if I can or even want to fight it, but for the most part, I want to fight it. I want to enjoy life and those around me. I want to grab those yellow experiences and treasure them.

In order to do this, I need to separate my struggles from who *I am*. There's a difference between accepting depression and anxiety as a trial in my life and believing that is who I am. **A *depressed* person is different from a *depressing* person.** A depressed person experiences depression. A depressing person intentionally or unintentionally makes others around them miserable.

I am someone who experiences depression and anxiety. Am I sometimes depressing? Do I sometimes cause unnecessary distress or frustration for those around me? Of course I do. But when I realize that's what I've done, I try to make amends, improve, and create a more positive environment.

The goal is to not *stay* stuck. That's it. We mustn't allow ourselves to stay stuck in the mud of our obstacles. Experience emotional drops, feel stuck and not know how to get out? Yes. But pushing forward and being willing to do hard things to become unstuck? YES!

If I believe the struggle of depression and anxiety is who I *am*, I am limited and find it more difficult to change. And if I deny that depression and anxiety exist in my life, I suppress my progress. I must face the darkness and call it what it is. Yes, this is a part of me, my life, and my experiences, but it does not need to define who I *am* or who I am *becoming*. That part is determined by God and by me.

Chapter 10

Just Don't Tell Grandmother

There Are Moments of Relief Awaiting Us

GRANDMOTHER WAS QUITE the proper lady. (That should be obvious by the fact we called her Grandmother instead of Grandma or some other Grandma-y name.) Yeah, she liked things a particular way. She lived about two hours away from us, and so we were able to visit her every once in a while.

An array of emotions—including nerves, excitement, and dread—cropped up during the drive to her house. After what felt like a long car ride, we were expected to go inside, say hi, and sit and visit for what felt like hours but was probably more like minutes. Grandmother sat precisely poised on her chair and asked us questions. She wasn't a very warm grandma. She also didn't believe in using any sugar, which I think qualifies as an official grandma crime.

Once we finally passed the grandmother interviews, my mom would dismiss us to play outside. That was like heaven in a biscuit. Oh, man. Grandmother had acres and acres of grass surrounded by acres and acres of woods. She had a massive

barn pigs had resided beneath decades earlier. And, oh, get this. She had a legitimate outhouse. And yes, we used it, but I don't think she ever found out . . .

She also had an old shop. It was a small building behind her house her dad used for work. Layers of dust covered piles of newspapers and letters inside the shop. We weren't allowed to go in—but, just like the outhouse, we decided not to tell her.

One day, my brothers and I were running stealth-like from the basement to the shop. As we ran over the large, old piece of wood laid across the ditch as a bridge to the shop's front door, the bridge suddenly busted and splintered. We didn't say a word. We avoided it and hoped she wouldn't notice.

Unfortunately, she did notice, and we were in big trouble. Lucky for us, there was not much we could do about it at the time, so we squirmed away after she scolded us and ran back outside. We were sooooo lucky! We continued to run through her massive yard, pick apples from her trees, and play in the barn.

Each time we visited Grandmother, we knew it would be difficult. We knew we had to get through the dreaded interviews before having any real fun. We knew dinnertime would be awful, but we also knew that playing in her cement-floored basement or her yard with all its fireflies would be worth it. It was our yellow.

———

My grandmother's yard was always miraculous. No matter how long the talks lasted or how scary the food was, there was always the yard. And it was always yellow. The more I understand that yellow is always there for us, the better I am able to push through the hard and become stronger.

Though we understandably wish we could consistently experience yellow, unfortunately, we don't have that choice. We must go inside and eat dinner—even if it's an atrocious tomato casserole (sorry, Grandmother). Even while experiencing things that typically bring us yellow, we will unintentionally destroy makeshift bridges. But let's not allow our repetitive cycles into darkness stop us from searching for yellow. The experience of yellow moments makes the fight worth it. Just remember that the more we actually fight with the knowledge that those yellow moments can and will occur for us, the more powerful we'll become.

Chapter 11

Is It a Target?!

The Process of Emotional Construction

I LIVE IN the suburbs, just far enough away from the city and close enough to the airport. It is constantly growing and being developed. Piles of lumber will suddenly materialize out of the blue—and we know what comes next. Dirt. Dust. Work crews. Caution signs. Immediately, we know it will be a zillion days until the project is complete and things get back to normal. Whether people are erecting new homes or widening roads, there is nonstop construction ahead.

As I watch things change, I actually get excited. I know . . . this may not be the typical response to construction. More often, people feel dread or frustration, which is completely understandable. It is aggravating to be in a hurry and not be able to get through the traffic. It's annoying when your view of the mountains gets blocked by another home. It's maddening when construction wakes you up too early in the morning. I get it.

It actually surprises me that construction makes me so excited. But whenever I see that machinery on-site, ready to dig and churn up the dirt, my imagination begins to stir. The guessing game has officially begun. Will we get to see a new home in the neighborhood as it emerges from the ground? Or are they widening the roads or adding a stoplight? Will we be getting a movie theater? A TARGET!?

Regardless of what's being built, construction means change. Something new and different is coming. It represents opportunity and growth. But just like we see the dust and piles of trash at a construction site, the construction of our lives can also be quite messy. While watching physical construction makes me excited and intrigued, emotional construction often makes me feel disheartened and hopeless. With emotional construction, it can be difficult and even impossible to see past the mess to the result.

Constructing a home requires so many steps, parts, and pieces that builders often feel overwhelmed by the details. Even before breaking ground, they need to learn all about the project and what it entails. Each step has to be planned out.

Lucky for us, emotional construction doesn't need to be such an arduous task. While it is true that seeing yellow takes time and effort, we can strive to simplify and broaden our search. **No matter how dark we might feel, we can search for and even find yellow during our construction process.**

Chapter 12

Blueprints Don't Have to Be Blue

We Determine What Our Emotional Construction Looks Like

IMAGINE YOUR DREAMIEST of dream homes. What would it look like? A modern farmhouse? A ranch-style house? What about on a lake with soaring windows that take in the view? Or maybe it's a cottage house right on the beach!

What would the inside look like? Would there be stairs to a second floor or basement? Would you be drawn to brighter colors, or would you keep it neutral? What space in your home would get the most attention as you are designing it?

Eventually, dreams for a new home have to make way for reality. Time and financial limitations crop up. So annoying. You need to seek the advice of skilled professionals, and, more than likely, do a lot of research. After getting a general idea of what you want, you may meet with someone to draw up the plans. Once plans are complete, money is settled, and contracts are signed, it's go time!

Typically, emotions fluctuate as the construction progresses. Some days involve more stress, some days less. You might find the inevitable construction bumps and detours testing your patience. You might feel chaos in all the mess. In fact, at times throughout the construction process, you might realize you have or haven't been realistic with your plans and money. Depending on which, you might have some very good days or some not-so-good days.

The whole idea of you building a home gets me excited! I would become instantly obsessed with your plans. I would want to see the images you have in mind. I'd want to dissect your blueprints and visually walk from room to room with you. I would be pumped to talk about why you chose to put this here and that there. It would fascinate me to picture what you have dreamed up and watch it take form. The growing, the developing, the *process* would be captivating and beautiful.

We end up learning lots about ourselves during the building process. We figure out whether we prefer to build quickly or slowly and whether we focus on the overall picture or the meticulous details.

My dream home is actually the one I live in. That might sound super cheesy, but it's true. When we bought it, there were holes in the stucco, and the carpet was worn. Over the years, we have added our own adventures and stories to it. It's had its share of food splatters on walls, fingerprints on windows, and broken glass. We've sat around the couch for hours on end laughing, crying, holding each other, and just being. Every day in this house is a new day filled with curves, bumps, dust, and noise.

Each one of us is building his or her own home. However, rather than it being a physical home with Sheetrock and paint, it's a metaphorical home built on past and current experiences. It holds our thoughts, feelings, trials, and beliefs.

Heavenly Father, the Savior, and we are the only ones who can see every corner of our homes. That's it. No matter how close we are to others, we are the only ones who have seen, felt, heard, and tasted every one of our experiences.

That means **it is up to us to determine how we are going to remodel our homes**. Did you catch that? It's up to *you*! Isn't that exciting? You may have walls in your homes that are difficult to tear down or cannot be torn down at all, but *you are the one who gets to decide what to do with them*!

I know, I know. It can be mind-boggling and maybe even feel paralyzing to know you are responsible for the outcome. Are there loading-bearing walls in every house that baffle and overwhelm us? Of course! But let's not forgo all remodeling because of those walls! Let's use them as an integral part of our design.

What if we took these walls of depression and anxiety, embraced them as part of our story, and made them as beautiful as possible? They would become ours. They would be void of shame. And, lo and behold, despite those enormous walls standing in front of us, we might begin to see flickering specks of yellow we didn't notice before.

Assessment

Looking at Where We Are
Emotionally, Physically,
and Spiritually
and Why

Chapter 13

I Don't See No Green

Looking for Relief in the Right Places

Moving to Arizona has been a bit of an adjustment. Though I lived in Utah and California for short periods, I was raised in North Carolina, where the landscape is completely different from Arizona's. The trees there actually change colors! Okay—I admit there are like two or three species of trees that change colors in Arizona, but, trust me, it is *not* the same. The

patches of grass here and there in Arizona do not compare to the
rolling hills and covered bridges of the South. Arizona's beauty
has been tough for me to find. Some say they love the cactus
and the Arizona mountains. To me, cacti are simply pokey and
unattractive, and the mountains look boring and naked.

While settling into Arizona, I started missing the massive,
shady trees and cool, damp grass of North Carolina. I craved
the woods behind our home and trails we'd created by raking
away leaves and sticks. I missed the old white church in those
woods where we played; we even attended Bible school there
once or twice. Nothing in Arizona seemed to compare.

I found myself in a bit of a pickle. I knew it was right for
our family to be in Arizona, yet I got disgusted whenever I
looked at the landscape. That probably sounds dramatic, but
it's true. I was looking for green. And not just any green but a
particular green. Here I was, in a different part of the country,
looking for a specific kind of beauty and feeling disappointed
when I couldn't find it. Nevertheless, the more I heard others
say Arizona was beautiful, the more curious I became. What
did they see? What was I missing? Did I even *want* to find or
admit there was beauty here?

As the years rolled by, I started paying more attention. And
guess what? It happened! Beauty started peeking around the

corner. I sat on the back porch and became enamored with the previously unfamiliar monsoon storms. Nothing had prepared me for such majestic thunder and lightning. And these sunsets? There are only two places where I've seen such brilliant sunsets. Hawaii and Arizona. That's it. Okay—I admit I haven't traveled all over the world to know if they are *the* absolute best, but trust me, they are stunning. An Arizona sunset can make you stop in your tracks, even if just for a second, to soak it in.

Before I found all this beauty, I had something very specific in mind—the way North Carolina looked—and I wouldn't

consider anything else. I had experienced a particular type of beauty, and I wanted that beauty again. Right then. But I wasn't looking for beauty in the right places.

When we crave relief and search for yellow, are we looking in the right place? Could we be missing fragments of yellow directly in front of us? Even in our darkest moments, God gives us yellow. This does *not* mean that as we experience deep pain, we are actually feeling peace and simply not noticing it. This also does *not* mean we should merely look at the bright side and get over our "issues."

What this does mean is that yellow is out there and God continues to give it to us. We may not recognize or feel yellow right now, but *that's okay.* As we continue to invite Him into our lives and begin to watch for yellow, He will reveal it to us, and we will be able to spot yellow even in our darkest moments.

God wants us to search for and find yellow. He wants to speak to us and reassure us that He is still there—that He has never left our side. In searching for and recognizing yellow, we confirm our faith that He is near. As a result, our testimonies remain solid regardless of whether we actually feel Him near. Spotting yellow may not completely take away the pain we wish we didn't understand, but it gives us the hope we so desperately need to push forward.

Chapter 14

What Shade Is It?

Finding Relief Is an Individualized Experience

REMEMBER HOW I was looking for the wrong shade of green in Arizona? Who knew the Arizona landscape would look so different from the one in North Carolina? Ha! Well, I find myself doing the same thing with yellow. Though there are a million shades of yellow, I often assume my yellow has to look the same as someone else's. I begin believing I will find peace, goodness, and hope the exact same way someone else finds theirs.

The temple, for example, can be such a great place of peace. Friends will often mention how they are struggling and need to go to the temple to regain the peace felt there. The peace I feel at the temple is more hit and miss depending on my emotional state. Assuming I should have the exact same experience as others brings all sorts of unsettling thoughts and emotions.

To search for *your* yellow, you must look in new places and watch for different shades than what you're used to. Searching for yellow is an invitation to pause, even for a split second.

Though it involves noticing things around us, it also means shifting, changing, and constructing. **When we determine to search for yellow, we are demanding a different story than what's right in front of us. We are deciding to fight with God by our side.**

The search for yellow is real, and doesn't come quickly and easily. How we experience yellow is unique to each of us. Our list of yellows will change, expand, and become tailored exclusively to us. And as we cultivate our personal yellows, they will become something we hold close to our hearts.

Searching for yellow . . .

- · Is personal
- · Requires us to dig deep
- · Means we are willing to change ourselves
- · Means we are willing to change our surroundings
- · Is difficult
- · Is repetitive
- · Is an evolving process
- · Requires change
- · Brings us closer to Christ

Searching for yellow is *not* . . .

- · The same for everyone
- · Looking at the bright side and getting over it
- · A quick fix

Ummmm . . . let's hope you don't hate the color yellow. That would be unfortunate, because, like it or not, you've got some yellow coming your way, baby!

Chapter 15

Hangin' with the Hippies

Planning Authentic Personal Goals

SURPRISE TRIPS MAY be the best invention ever. Though it's become a tad bit trickier since airport security has increased, surprise trips are still possible. And they're fabulous. Years ago, I decided to surprise my husband for his birthday. Since he didn't have a clue as to where we were headed, I had to help him a bit with packing the right stuff.

After some finagling through luggage check-in and security, we arrived at the gate, where our departure to San Francisco was announced. My husband quickly got excited and was ready for a long weekend of visiting the Golden Gate Bridge and driving down Lombard Street.

We landed at the San Francisco airport and got off the plane. While still in the terminal, I began to wander a bit and linger around. He became confused and probably assumed I was trying to dramatize the surprise.

Soon, boarding was called for Eureka, California, and I pulled out our additional plane tickets. He was shocked. He laughed as we walked out onto the tarmac and climbed the stairs to a tiny jet plane. He had no clue where Eureka was, and he became more intrigued by the minute. And he was dumbfounded when the plane was full of hippies! Little did we know we would be spending the whole weekend with these folks! (Side note . . . How in the world do they get dreads all the way to the ground? Do they use extensions? It's a real question, people.)

The plane landed, and we disembarked. We walked into the puny terminal, where we were greeted by a "Welcome to the Redwoods" sign. Yup, we had flown to the Redwoods. Visiting a redwood forest had been on my husband's bucket list for years. Though it was different from what he first assumed, the ultimate destination was a big hit!

For some reason, life never turns out as we have planned. My kids tell me exactly what their futures will look like, and I just smile. Having said that, I fully encourage them to set goals. Though we end up with unexpected bumps and bruises along the way, the more we plan, the more likely we are to hit our objectives.

Even with the restrictions of living with depression and anxiety, **we should create and live by realistic, positive, and motivating goals**—goals that give us identity and purpose. Think about what drives you. Do your goals encourage progress and success? Are they optimistic? It has taken me awhile to determine my goals, but I think I finally have them pinpointed!

They include:

1. Live the happiest, fullest life possible
2. Never give up on finding hope, peace, and true joy
3. Have as many yellow experiences as possible
4. Don't beat myself up emotionally
5. Love myself

Do these seem too obvious or basic? They might to you. But for me, they are deeply personal and powerful. I feel them passionately in my bones. Authentic personal goals give us greater opportunities for success. Rather than staying stuck in a rut, when we have goals that inspire us, we become anxious to progress.

Chapter 16

The Catalyst

Pinpointing What Motivates Us

I ASSUME THE majority of Arizonians, including me, take the monsoons and sunsets for granted. Seasons go by without any of us noticing. We may even forget about them entirely until suddenly they catch us off guard once again.

I find myself doing this exact thing when it comes to looking for yellow moments in my life. Especially when I'm experiencing depression and anxiety, it can seem impossible to find beauty or peace anywhere. The stress, fear, and gloom become all-consuming. Emotional survival becomes paramount, and it doesn't seem possible to focus on anything else.

That forces the question: What is it that truly drives us?

Are our motives embedded deep enough in our hearts that they push us forward? We must feel there is a true purpose for us if we are to push ourselves and find yellow. What makes it worth searching for yellow? Why are we fighting?

If you decide you are gonna look for the relief of yellow to be "happier," you may want to rethink that motive. When in the depths of depression, we might not care less if we ever will be happy again. When depressed, darkness and pain can feel strangely comfortable. Pushing past this bleak comfort takes more than simply wanting relief. If our motives are not specific and genuinely personal, we should consider vamping and revamping those motives until we find ones that speak to us and give us the strength to fight for yellow.

Let there be no confusion. Each and every time I struggle, I feel stuck, and the thought of changing *anything* makes me sick to my stomach. I feel beaten down. The whole emotional process seems daunting, and it's difficult to comprehend a different outcome than the harsh reality I am currently experiencing. And, honestly, I often want to simply sit in my mess. It becomes a comfortable place where I prefer to linger rather than face the harder task of fighting it.

You'd think we would always want to fight for happiness and peace because we are worth it. But when consumed by depression and anxiety, do we even feel worth fighting for? Worth is something I have struggled with all my life. I am definitely in a better place than I used to be, but it is one of the demons that regularly pop in and out of my life. Don't get me wrong; I deeply believe in the principle of infinite self-worth. I see it around me, genuinely feel it for others, and I think others see worth in me. Prophets have consistently and repeatedly taught us of our worth. Just ask, and they'll tell you that no matter what you have done, no matter who you are, you are of infinite worth. That's it. No strings attached.

As children of God, we are taught that we have infinite worth no matter what. But do we truly believe and feel it? Well, it's easier to say it than to actually believe and feel it. If we waited to search for yellow until we felt good about ourselves, we might never begin.

Admittedly, we need to be motivated to push ourselves forward. So, what kinds of motivations can help? Those that have helped me include:

- I want to be there for my family as much as I possibly can each day.
- I want to learn how to cope so that I might help others going through similar trials.
- I want to make the best of hard circumstances.
- I want to be proud of myself for doing hard things.
- I want to be an example to those around me.
- I want others to have positive memories of me.
- I refuse to allow my struggles to be an excuse for how I treat others.
- I want to always remember that pushing through the hard makes the yellow experiences that much sweeter.

Personally established motivations are the catalysts for us to fight against the dark and begin our search for the yellow. For our motivations to be truly effective, they must be genuine and come from deep within us. Dig deep with me and identify what motivates you. What makes it worth it for you to fight for yellow?

Chapter 17

Hash It Out

Facing Obstacles That Hinder Us from Finding Relief

MY DAD SUFFERED from bipolar disorder his entire adult life. It was not only all-consuming for him but for those around him. It was a constant guessing game as to where he was emotionally. I've met numerous people with bipolar disorder, and I must say that my dad was different. His bipolar disorder wasn't the issue. The issue was that he didn't own his actions. He would unapologetically say what was on his mind regardless of how it impacted anyone else.

I lived in a world of contradictions. I was overly sensitive and felt that few people understood me. I felt stupid, abnormal, and idiotic. I felt unattractive and annoying. As I battled these ideas, I heard others talk about my intelligence, beauty, and worth. I was blessed to be surrounded by those who loved and supported me, but I was completely confused.

I don't necessarily think my dad wanted to destroy my self-esteem, but, unfortunately, it's one of the things I've struggled with. I

#SKILLS

became pretty good at internalizing the negative and pushing away the positive.

I remember the day. I was fed up. I had had enough of the belittling and criticisms. No matter what I did or how I helped, it was never enough. But I knew I deserved something better. Kindness, respect, apologies, appreciation. Something. Anything.

While he was in the hospital one time, he began telling me I wasn't capable of understanding the issues he had with the rehabilitation nurses. Something in me clicked. For the first time, I stood up for myself. I let him know enough was enough. My husband stood by my side as I released the pent-up feelings and hurt I'd kept inside for years. I told him I deserved respect and kindness.

We then left my dad's hospital room and walked out.

After so many years of pain, I couldn't believe I'd stood up to him. And you know what? It was horrible. Nevertheless, relief came, albeit slowly. It took months before I felt confident about what I had done.

I had many more years with my dad before he passed away. I can't say they were good, but they were better. At least I was better. I was beginning to understand my worth and was able to sift through what had been affecting me.

My experiences with my dad were major obstacles to finding yellow. I've had to sort through the things that happened and figure out why they bothered me, where my thoughts would take me, and what I have hung on to. Connecting the dots has not been easy.

———

Recognizing my triggers as well as how certain past experiences have affected me has been a pain. I mean, who wants to sift through all their dirt? Not me! However, to understand why I act a certain way in certain situations, I've had to go there. I've had to do that sifting.

Triggers, current experiences, and genetics can all be obstacles to finding yellow. What's the danger? We can become consumed or hindered by these obstacles, and we may be tempted to feel sorry for ourselves and threaten to stay stuck in our mess rather than use any new knowledge to progress.

We must assess our obstacles with the goal of learning from what we discover. Sifting then becomes an opportunity to understand how to approach triggers and obstacles. We become more aware of who we are, why we react in certain ways, and how we want (or need) to change. And we are better equipped to tackle any more obstacles inevitably thrown our way.

What are some of the obstacles in your life? Can any of them be altered or eliminated by changing your:

- Physical environment (who or what you're surrounded by)
- Spiritual environment (ridding yourself of bad habits and doing what you can to invite Christ)
- Thought processes (negative thoughts or belief systems)

———

It frustrates me that even as an adult, I've continued to carry my experiences with my dad like a weight around my neck.

Though I am better able to recognize triggers from my child-hood, I wish this struggle would simply go away.

Since my dad's passing, my heart has begun to soften. There were good moments with him, and I try to remember those. I will never know what he truly experienced in mor-tality; he may very well have done the best he could. Maybe the only thing I consistently wish is that I would have begun my search for yellow earlier. I have always *wanted* yellow and even *looked* for yellow, but I wish I would have started actively *searching* sooner. Had I realized he was probably doing the best he could, and had I actively begun searching for yellow, maybe my experiences with him wouldn't have continued to hit me so hard as an adult.

Though I can't change the past, I can change my future. **My job is to learn from what I have been given and improve *myself*.**

Chapter 18

What's It Worth?

The Difficulty of Feeling
We Are Worth Fighting For

A COUPLE OF years ago, I was asked to help with a small, private luncheon. Elder Jeffrey R. Holland was coming to visit our stake, and we were to feed him between meetings. As the time for the luncheon grew closer, I started caving emotionally. I deeply wanted to feel I was worthy enough to be in Elder Holland's presence, but the self-deprecating voices in my head were loud. An Apostle of the Lord was coming, and I was completely absorbed in my own lack of self-worth.

I teetered between depression and anxiety. One moment I was consumed with darkness; the next, my heart would race. And Satan took advantage of my depression and anxiety, attempting to destroy any strength I had by further tearing me down.

How could I even be in the same room with Elder Holland? My soul felt as if my every imperfection would be exposed. With tears in my eyes, I emotionally collapsed in front of my friend Aly. She consoled and encouraged me. Though I was embarrassed by my drama, she gave me the strength and insight I needed to believe in myself.

The luncheon came, and it was a beautiful moment of bright yellow. I served Elder Holland and was able to stay and listen when he spoke to the local leaders. Through the Spirit, I was told that God loved me and I hadn't been completely ridiculous for freaking out about a luncheon. God understood me and my insecurities, doubts, and emotional pain.

Since that luncheon, I have often wondered how different things would have been if I had felt confidence in the Lord. Maybe, just maybe, if I had chosen to believe in the Lord's love for me earlier, it would have been a much less emotionally unsettling process.

What's funny is that the worth of the others in the room didn't even cross my mind. How is it we can feel so lonely in a world filled with billions of people? We believe in a loving Heavenly Father and a Savior who died for each of us. We look at others and can't fathom they would ever feel unloved or alone. We convince ourselves we are the only ones experiencing or deserving of such agony and emptiness.

Ironically, Elder Holland speaks often of our worth and counsels us not to be discouraged. He addresses mental health issues and encourages us to press forward with faith in Christ.

He reminds us we are loved and never alone. At the October 2013 general conference, President Thomas S. Monson made a similar statement when he said,

> Your Heavenly Father loves you—each of you. That love never changes. It is not influenced by your appearance, by your possessions, or by the amount of money you have in your bank account. It is not changed by your talents and abilities. It is simply there. It is there for you when you are sad or happy, discouraged or hopeful. God's love is there for you whether or not you feel you deserve love. It is simply always there . . . we do not ever walk alone. I promise you that you will one day stand aside and look at your difficult times, and you will realize that He was always there beside you.

If we trust Heavenly Father and His prophets, shouldn't we try to believe His prophets when they tell us He loves us and is there for us? What if we based our life, goals, purpose, motivation, happiness, and progression on the belief that as children of God, we are invaluable and He will never leave us? What if each morning, we could make decisions with the understanding that He is aware of us, cares for us, and loves us even as we experience the dark void of depression and loneliness.

That said, *believing* **God loves us is very different from** *feeling* **that love.** I find it easier to accept and *believe* He loves me rather than actually *feel* His love. Feeling His love requires recognizing it, experiencing it, and embracing it. It requires not only accepting His love but actually being able to enjoy the peace that comes with it. This seems to be a considerably more difficult task. Could it be possible that we do not recognize His love or Spirit because of our depression and anxiety?

Chapter 19

The Promise

He Has Not Left Us
Even When We Can't Feel His Spirit

HERE'S THE DEAL. It took me years to come to grips with the following concept: *When I am struggling with depression and/or anxiety, I cannot feel the Spirit. I also do not feel God's love.* Because I struggled to feel His love, I figured I must be making mistakes I wasn't aware of or that I wasn't worth His time. I thought His Spirit had left me. I assumed He simply didn't love me as much as He loved everyone else.

It was confusing, frustrating, and spiritually draining, and it made me angry and added to the piercing loneliness of my darkest moments. Was this a cruel game? Why couldn't I feel peace or hope even after praying and receiving blessings? What was the point? What kind of awful human was I to be punished like this? Was it to humble or test me? It became embarrassing and demoralizing.

Repeated cycles of ups and downs over the years have allowed me to recognize that the yellow *does* come, though it's never as soon as I want it to. Fortunately, during the welcomed yellow, I do find I am able to recognize Him and feel His Spirit again. In the April 2016 general conference, Elder Holland quotes President George Q. Cannon, saying,

> No matter how serious the trial, how deep the distress, how great the affliction, *[God] will never desert us. He never has, and He never will.* He cannot do it. It is not His character [to do so]. . . . He will [always] stand by us. We may pass through the fiery furnace; we may pass through deep waters; but. . . .We shall emerge from all these trials and difficulties the better and purer for them.

What a relief it is to know He has not left us after all. And because of that, through this nightmare, we will improve and become stronger! How blessed we are to have Him with us always. **We may not be able to *feel* Him, but He will not *leave* us.** He is there!

———

I used to believe that if Heavenly Father really was beside me, I would recognize His presence. Admittedly, there have been a few times when I was at my darkest and He blessed me with glimpses of yellow. But that has been rare.

While we are in the middle of depression and anxiety, intense emotional blocks are created. Our minds become foggy and muddled. We go into survival mode, and connection with the Spirit feels either limited or nonexistent.

This is not the ideal time to evaluate ourselves spiritually. It's the time to choose: What do we want? Do we want to give up, or do we want to push ourselves to feel His Spirit again? At this point, through trial and error, I have found hope to be my best friend—not blind hope but hope built on previous experience. Hope I can feel peace and comfort as I have before.

Hope that as I push to design and rebuild myself, the yellow will shine into my home as well as my heart.

He wants us to search for and find Him. He wants us to continue to talk to Him even when we can't feel Him. He stays by our side and waits patiently for us to push toward the impending yellow. Once we are able to feel His Spirit again, He comforts us and reminds us He never left. He hurts when we hurt, and He loves us no matter what phase of construction we're in.

Don't give up on Him. Let go of the guilt when you can't feel His Spirit. Push for the yellow where His Spirit dwells. Even when you can't feel it, He is there and has promised to never give up on you.

Chapter 20

Thorn in Our Side

The Manipulations and Tricks of Satan

I'VE FAILED AGAIN.
I wanna give up.
I'm not worth fighting for.
God has left me anyway.
It's too hard.
It's embarrassing.

These are all thoughts I battle with. I know they are negative, but they keep recurring, especially when I struggle. Although it makes sense that Heavenly Father wouldn't want His children to think this way about themselves, these negative statements feel so accurate, so real.

Where do these thoughts come from? It's confusing. I've wondered how unrighteous I must be to believe such things about myself—to "allow Satan into my mind."

———

Satan is our biggest opponent. He is sneaky and deceptive. He wants us to be angry about our lives and our trials and with those around us. He wants us to use depression and anxiety as excuses to bulldoze and damage others without any feelings of accountability. He wants us to feel hopeless and discouraged.

Satan wants us to believe God has abandoned us. He manipulates and tricks us to make us angry toward God because of our trials. He hopes we will lose our testimonies and even deny the existence of our Heavenly Father and Christ.

Satan enjoys disrupting any search for yellow. He relishes in us looking for answers and peace without the guidance of our Heavenly Father. He takes advantage of our search for relief and twists the truth while attempting to steer us in the wrong direction.

We tend to believe Satan's lies about who we are—*I am nothing; I am a failure; I can't progress*—when we're in the midst of depression and anxiety because we aren't thinking straight. When these kinds of damming thoughts repeatedly invade our minds, we begin to believe them. We welcome these deceptions as truths.

Satan wants to take advantage of our struggles and add to our misery. His goal is to undermine any attempt we make to move forward. We must stay alert to these deceptions as we choose what to believe about ourselves.

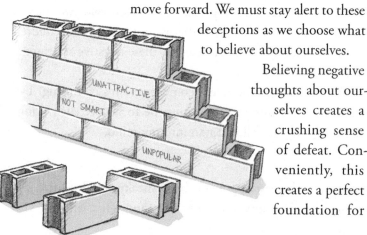

Believing negative thoughts about ourselves creates a crushing sense of defeat. Conveniently, this creates a perfect foundation for a solid wall preventing us from moving forward. Satan's goal in reinforcing that wall is to cripple us.

And unfortunately, we often reinforce that wall even when others plead for us to stop. Our wall becomes a structure that torments us, yet we leave it standing. We find clever ways to justify building and maintaining our wall, and we believe it is built on a foundation of truth. Words of love, support, and encouragement find no place within the wall we have built. But here's what we don't realize: there is light and truth just beyond the wall.

Satan knows that the more he can cripple us, the better. As members of the Church, we sometimes assume we must believe these self-defeating thoughts to prevent ourselves from becoming prideful.

Recognizing where these negative thoughts come from is a game changer. When we finally see them for the lies they are, we can set them aside. Refusing to believe the adversary allows us to begin to love ourselves and be more accepting of who we are. It opens a window for us to hear the whisperings and encouragement of the Holy Ghost. It allows further opportunities for us to feel the relieving balm of yellow.

It's normal while experiencing something as dark as depression or anxiety for it to seem impossible for us to feel the Spirit or see any yellow in our lives. Satan would have us believe we aren't good enough or righteous enough to feel Heavenly Father's Spirit. But let me be clear. Not being able to feel the Spirit does not equate to being unrighteous.

There's confusion between Satan's influence and the impact of depression and anxiety. **Satan and depression/anxiety are separate things.** We can be influenced by Satan even when not suffering from depression or anxiety. We can also experience depression or anxiety without being influenced by Satan. Or we can be in the depths of depression and anxiety *and* get hit by Satan and his tactics. Never forget that Satan will attack us when we're down.

My friend Jonathan describes depression and anxiety as "loud emotions." I think that's spot on. Satan takes these "loud emotions" and adds to them. Though it is understandably important to recognize Heavenly Father's Spirit in our lives, it can be equally as important to be aware of Satan's influence. Identifying this is empowering. As I have worked to create awareness of what my depression and anxiety look like versus Satan and his tactics, I have been surprised to realize how often Satan is working on me.

Still, it can be difficult to differentiate between depression/anxiety and Satan's influence. Both are negative, dark, and can make us feel lonely and hopeless. They drag us down and prevent our progress. Both are places I don't want to be, but sometimes I can't avoid them. In trying to recognize what I am experiencing, I have found the following things helpful:

1. I recognize that depression/anxiety are different from the adversary's influence.

2. I recognize that he is probably going to attack me while I'm down.

3. I decide not to let him win.

4. I pray for strength to fight against him so I can focus more intently on my current struggle against depression/anxiety.

5. I recognize that the Lord wants to help me even when I can't feel Him near.

6. I focus on inviting the Spirit and doing something about my negative thoughts/feelings—for example, I might go to the doctor or speak with a loved one.

7. I decide to push for yellow no matter what.

Satan's biggest goal is to damn and deter us from finding peace and happiness. Anything he can do to stop us from feeling the Spirit is a success for him. He doesn't care that we are struggling; he wants us to fail. To him, the more miserable we are, the better. We gain spiritual and emotional strength when we recognize his negative and stifling influence. Our search for yellow becomes our ammunition.

The more we search for it, the more we invite the Lord into our lives and free ourselves from the adversary's influence. We develop an awareness of Christ and strengthen our testimonies. We close the door to hopelessness and begin to open the window of relief from our emotional pain.

Chapter 21

The Perfect Disaster

The Cultural Pressures of Perfection

PERIODICALLY, THE CULTURAL pressure in the Church will make me wonder if I am doing any good at all. I don't mean to sound extreme, but at times that culture can be quite heavy. For example, I often experience emotional lows during and after general conference. When others share how uplifted they feel after watching conference, I wonder what's wrong with me.

Between my insecurities and depression and anxiety, attending church and watching general conference can feel like an attack on me. It can be a constant fight to figure out whether Heavenly Father is trying to tell me to work on something, whether Satan is attacking me, or whether I am having a bout of depression. During the general conference of April 2016, Elder Holland said,

> The gospel, the Church, and these wonderful semi-annual gatherings are intended to give hope and inspiration. *They are not intended to discourage you.* Only the adversary, the enemy of us all, would try to convince us that the ideals outlined in general conference

are depressing and unrealistic, that people don't really improve, that no one really progresses.

With the gift of the Atonement of Jesus Christ and the strength of heaven to help us, we can improve, and the great thing about the gospel is *we get credit for trying, even if we don't always succeed.*

Please remember tomorrow, and all the days after that, that the Lord *blesses those who want to improve.* . . . If you stumble in that pursuit, so does everyone; *the Savior is there to help you keep going.* (Emphasis added.)

What a relief to know I must not be the only one who struggles with general conference and other church meetings. If we do become overwhelmed and discouraged, Elder Holland reminds us that this is actually Satan trying to tear us down.

Despite my difficulties with church and general conference, I have also had beautiful yellow experiences where the speakers touched my heart and uplifted and inspired me. In order to obtain more of these positive experiences, I pray for strength and strive to fight the negative as I listen for speakers that touch my heart. I pay attention to the positive little pings in my soul and allow them to become treasures. During talks when I am racked with guilt, I try to assess whether the Lord is encouraging me to do better or Satan is taking advantage of my insecurities.

We are imperfect beings who are asked to try our best. That's it. We are to do our very best with what we have been given. I love how Elder Holland says we get credit for trying. Isn't that fantastic? Heavenly Father knows exactly what we are facing and what we are capable of. Our challenge is to acknowledge our trials and face them head-on, all while doing our best to stay close to the Lord along the way. As we do so, the Savior will be by our side. How incredible is that?

Why is it that my neighbor's lawn is always green? I never see chunks of stucco missing on my neighbor's house, either. I bet they have a garden with plants that are actually alive. Super annoying.

I'm sure they never yell at their kids, and they probably listen to uplifting music throughout the week. They're as close to perfect as one can get. I can't imagine they've ever experienced insecurity, much less depression or anxiety. I wish they weren't so nice. I'd really like to hate them, dang it.

I've found that comparing myself to others is *not* helpful. Ha! Go figure. Not that I try to be unappreciative of my blessings or what I've been given; that's not it. Rather, it's more that I used to be a bit naive about the struggles others faced behind closed doors. There is a false belief that others must not experience hard like we do. And that's quite damning to us.

It's actually a beautiful, eye-opening experience to see that everyone has their own hard. Obviously, I would *never* wish hard on anyone. However, it's refreshing to know we are not alone. It changes how we see those around us. We can appreciate their strengths and love them in the midst of their trials—even if we don't know what those trials are.

Oh. I forgot to mention that my neighbor's lawn is turf. Hmmm. Maybe that's why it's always green.

———

As members of the Church, we frequently hear about the concept of perfection. We form ideas of what ideal life looks like and judge ourselves by that standard. Are we good enough or righteous enough? Sometimes we create these lofty ideals. Other times, these ideals are perpetuated by Church culture—not doctrine but culture.

It can be confusing since the ideals we uphold are typically admirable. But we encounter problems when we take these ideals to an excess and create unrealistic expectations for ourselves. We end up with an impossible view of what we need to do or be for Heavenly Father to love us, for us to love ourselves, or to simply feel of worth at all. To add insult to injury, when we don't live up to all those impossible expectations, we feel as if we are failures to God and/or ourselves.

Goals:
- No Depression
- No Anxiety
- Never get upset
- Keep everything clean
- Never fear
- Always keep calm

But perfection is the goal, right? No! *Immediate* perfection is *not* the goal. The goal is *eventual* perfection. It has taken awhile for me to truly understand this concept. Our goal is to be consistently trying, continually improving. **Our goal is *progress*.** At the October 2006 general conference, Relief Society General President Bonnie Parkin said,

> Do we think we have to be perfect in order to deserve His love? When we allow ourselves to feel "encircled about eternally in the arms of his love," we feel safe, and we realize that we don't need to be immediately perfect. We must acknowledge that perfection is a process. This is a gospel of eternal progress, and we must remember to appreciate the journey.

Though I am still learning to appreciate my journey with depression and anxiety, I can respect the concept. I want to learn and improve. I don't want to stay stuck in the same place and repeat unnecessary challenges that can be avoided. I am beginning to recognize things I am learning from my trials, such as:

- Trusting the Lord's timing
- Managing my thoughts and actions
- Understanding how Heavenly Father speaks to me
- Understanding how Satan tears me down
- Feeling empathy
- Experiencing accountability

I definitely don't *want* to experience depression and anxiety, but I have begun to appreciate the lessons I continue to learn. As this trial persists and I focus on what I am learning from it, it becomes more bearable. Rather than comparing myself to others or to some imagined perfect ideal, I compare myself to where I have been, how much I have fought, what I have learned, and how far I've come.

Recognizing the progress that's come as a result of our trials helps with the false concept that we need to be perfect *now*. We are not currently at the point of perfection, but we can be on the path that leads there. Then, when the time comes, we can be fully perfected through Christ.

———

But our progress is stopped when we believe our depression and anxiety signify failure. In the face of these self-identified failures, we assume we must be way off the path to perfection. We suppose others must be on the path to perfection without us.

We can be battling depression and anxiety and struggling with feeling His Spirit and still be on the path toward eventual perfection. The trick is to find a balance between **accepting our challenge** of depression/anxiety and **recognizing Satan's voice** while consistently **pushing ourselves to improve and inviting the Lord into our lives.**

If we are not careful, we may find ourselves using our struggles as excuses. For example, we may decide that since immediate perfection is not the goal, we don't need to do our darndest. We may decide that we cannot live a fulfilling life while suffering from depression or anxiety. We may convince ourselves that inviting the Lord to be in our lives while we are struggling is impossible.

Don't allow depression or anxiety to pull you into that trap. Refuse to believe you will never feel the Spirit or enjoy church or general conference again. Don't let Satan convince you that you're not worth it, that you can't or won't ever see yellow. Refuse to wait to feel the Lord and His calming power.

Instead, push for yellow. Be honest with yourself and your struggles and accept them for what they are. Be willing to tear down or work around the walls that may get in your way. Strive for eventual perfection, recognizing that it's a process. Begin to love yourself. Trust that despite the trials, you will be able to feel joy again. Embrace Christ's infinite love and mercy and believe in His unwavering love for you, even in your darkest moments.

Chapter 22

Connecting the Dots

Recognizing Depression and Anxiety Patterns

DEPRESSION AND ANXIETY can so dominate our lives that they affect everything we do, from sleeping and eating to how we think about and react to the world around us. Depression and anxiety can manipulate additional aspects of our lives, such as how we pray or read the scriptures. If we aren't mindful of what is truly happening, we may even begin to assume God has left us. This can chip away at or even destroy our testimonies.

So far, depression and anxiety have been a continual part of my life. But as I continue to search for yellow, I have noticed patterns. For example, someone treating me as if I am stupid can quickly trigger depression. Going to a social event when already highly anxious can trigger a panic attack.

These patterns are intimately connected to my story, past experiences, triggers, and testimony. The patterns, though sometimes consistent, can also be fluid. Sometimes they change. This transformation used to be discouraging until I alized that my experiences can change as I change. That's my goal! My goal is movement. My goal is progression.

Connecting the dots between and becoming more aware of our experiences and reactions to them not only opens our eyes but can also be healing. It allows us to understand how we respond to the effects of depression and anxiety in our lives. We can begin to determine how long we have been in a low and pinpoint how much or little we need to push ourselves. The more we assess, the more we will know what to tell doctors, therapists, and loved ones as we seek their help.

Connecting the dots in this way can help us understand why we may or may not be feeling the Spirit. It also gives us an inkling as to how long it may be until we feel it again (unless we have a lucky streak!). Meanwhile, we can be fortified with patience and strength as we look forward to feeling His Spirit again.

Since the effects of depression and anxiety are so encompassing, it can be difficult to wrap our minds around it all. As a lover of spreadsheets and all things visually mapped out, I have found that using charts helps me more clearly understand myself. Looking at the charts, I am able to more distinctly recognize the level of depression and/or anxiety I am experiencing as well as how much I need to push myself to move beyond it.

There's another purpose to the spreadsheet madness. I tend to block out the lows once they have passed. That may not seem like a bad thing, but when such an experience happens again, unless I'm aware of what I have previously experienced and the patterns in relation to my anxiety or depression, I can be blindsided.

Spreadsheets also prevent me from feeling quite so discouraged when I *can't* push myself further. Referring to past experiences reminds me that it's okay to have times when I feel I absolutely can't move forward right then. It allows me to accept the "non-searching for yellow" days and not beat myself up for taking a break from the fight. From the information in my spreadsheets, I can see that there is still hope for the relief of yellow, even though I don't feel it at the time.

Each chart you'll find in the chapters below includes various levels of depression (mild, moderate, severe, suicidal, numb) and anxiety (mild, moderate, severe, panic attack, anxiety fog). In the depression charts, *numb* is the defense mechanism that can be our go-to when overwhelmed. It feels as if we have no emotion. We don't care about things we normally would.

Anxiety fog is also a defense mechanism, but it feels a bit different than being numb. Anxiety fog makes it difficult to think straight and can vary from mild to severe enough that we need to hyper focus to do even the most basic things, such as pressing the gas pedal.

As we dive into a view of my behind-closed-doors life, feel free to compare it to your own. You might even consider looking at my charts, circling the similarities between my life and yours, and crossing out differences.

Here we go. You'll get a look into the life of a girl who, as a member of the Church, lives with depression and anxiety but continues to search for her yellow.

A Day in the Life

Chapter 23

Easy as Pie?

Thought Process

A JOB POPPED up in the bakery of a nearby restaurant. They were looking for someone to learn how to make umpteen specialty pies. Given my impressive talent for serving food in a college cafeteria, I was obviously highly qualified for such a task!

I shadowed others and received training. I lived pies for days and loved it! Then came the big day. It was time for me to showcase my mean pie-making skills. As two coworkers stood and talked on the other side of the bakery, I dug in. Soon, something didn't seem  right, but I couldn't pinpoint what it was. I continued working as the girls talked.

After a period of time, I asked the girls where the cornstarch was. They looked at me and started laughing. It wasn't just a giggle. It was a make-fun-of laugh. Apparently, I had mistaken the cornstarch for flour. They dumped out my efforts. I was humiliated.

Each day at work became worse. I was treated as if I were a joke. I felt stupid and emotionally worn. I dreaded going to work and became embarrassed about who I was. The joy of my new job rapidly evaporated, and it became difficult for me to even get out of bed. At the time, I couldn't figure out why I was so miserable.

Before long, I ran into someone I had worked with at my previous job. They happened to be looking for a cook and asked if I would consider coming back. Needless to say, I left the previously coveted pie job and went where I felt loved and accepted.

Our thoughts can be our biggest demons or our best friends. I am always amazed at how quickly they can spiral out of control. How in the world can we go from feeling secure and confident to barely being able to get out of bed? At times, it can feel as if our minds are stuck and all we can do is survive.

Obviously, our environment contributes a great deal to our thought processes. In my short-lived pie job, I was triggered by others mocking me. Their criticisms overshadowed any of the good things happening at work. I quickly found myself in a dark place where I believed everything they said.

Some of the most powerful clues as to how we are doing emotionally include what thoughts we are having as well as how quickly those thoughts are changing. Thoughts can be our most valuable tool in preventing or slowing a spiral. The sooner we can catch spiraling, negative thoughts, the better.

What are those thoughts, and where are they coming from? Are they truthful, helpful, and necessary? We will continue to cycle through habitual thoughts until we interrupt this damaging routine through personal assessment and/or therapy.

It is paramount that we monitor our thoughts as well as how they are affecting our decisions and lives. We can determine right from wrong, positive from negative, healing from damaging when it comes to our thoughts. We can begin to figure out where they stem from and in what direction they're sending us. This takes effort and dedication, but the results are invaluable.

A Note of Caution: As you become aware of your thoughts, try not to become discouraged. Breaking habits of thought takes time and work. Be patient with yourself. (My therapist is laughing at me now because I am still working on this.) But for reals. Don't get stuck on finding fault with yourself; instead, look for understanding and opportunities to grow. Below are charts of what my thoughts might look like at the various stages of depression and anxiety.

Thought Process
Depression

Mild	I struggle with self-worth but feel like the Lord still loves me. I'm able to review and access past experiences in order to strive for continual learning and growth.
Moderate	I experience on-and-off self-bashing but feel strong enough to combat it most of the time. I feel the Lord's love, but I assume He is annoyed with my constant struggle. I'm very aware of triggers, so I don't drop further. I feel lots of guilt for not being a better person.

(continued on next page)

Severe	I'm overwhelmed. My thoughts are negative and all-consuming. This is emotional-survival mode. It feels as if a weight is physically and emotionally pressing down on me. It feels like everyone hates me. I feel worthless and am consumed with self-deprecation. A degree of paranoia sets in as I think others can read my thoughts and "sense" my emotions. I experience strong guilt for not being a better or emotionally stronger person.
Suicidal	I feel everyone would be better without me around. I feel I cause issues with everything and everyone. I couldn't care less about how I treat others because I want to prove they are better off without me. I envision what life would be like for others without me. I have very dark and scary but convincing thoughts. I want to give up on everything. I can't see any light at the end of the tunnel. I think about the quickest and/or simplest way for me to not have to live anymore. I am overcome with darkness.
Numb	It's as if my emotions have been deleted from my mind. There is a disconnect from the world around me. There is no excitement, no fear, no sadness. It's as if I am emotionally paralyzed. I feel frozen and incapable of making decisions. I don't want to care about anything or anyone around me. Making decisions seems nearly impossible.

Thought Process
Anxiety

Mild	My senses are heightened, but I can think clearly enough to make decisions. I am proud that I can handle the current issue. I am fairly comfortable with what others think of me. I stay somewhat cautious and aware of my environment. I may have skeptical thoughts, but my perception of reality is mostly clear.

(continued on next page)

Moderate   My senses are heightened, and I can't think quite as clearly. I think mainly about the issue at hand. It becomes harder for me to think about others' needs. I tend to overthink and overanalyze. I become worried about what others think about me. I have heightened concerns and doubts about myself. I feel as if my emotions are teetering and I'm vulnerable. Confidence comes only in small spurts. My perception of what big or small problems entail is distorted. I am more self-focused than I would like to be in order to control emotions. I fluctuate in my ability to think straight.

Severe   My senses are heightened, and I can't think straight. I feel overwhelmed and consumed with the issues in front of me. I feel stupid, negative, and hopeless. I worry about what others think of me and become consumed with thinking the worst. I feel completely alone, convinced others are thinking and talking bad about me. I feel as if I am over the edge. My brain feels empty. It is intensely difficult to communicate how I'm feeling. I become very defensive, and my perception of reality is skewed. I am very self-focused.

Panic Attack   I feel confused as to what is happening. I have feelings of hopelessness. I am less worried about what the world thinks of me because I am consumed with my current situation. I recognize I am over the edge and attempt to give myself time and patience to get back on track.

Anxiety Fog   My mind goes blank; oftentimes, I forget what I was talking about, what I was doing, or how to do something. It can take extra brainpower to do the simplest things, such as driving.

Chapter 24

He Is Still There

Feeling His Spirit

IT WAS A tender mercy when we found out my brother Daniel would be headed to the MTC two weeks before college started. We could fly out west together, drop him off at the MTC, and then I could stay with relatives until the dorms opened. I had never been on a plane before, so I was quite anxious and was glad we would be flying together.

He had me sit near the window and sat calmly beside me. It was quite unnerving to feel the plane accelerating, and I seemed to be the only one who was the least bit bothered. Daniel talked and joked with me, soothing me as the plane took off. We laughed as I caught my breath with nervous anxiety and watched the plane lift off the ground. He was there with me the whole day. I could feel his comfort and guidance throughout our time at the airport and on the plane. He was my yellow.

Unfortunately, we had to drop him off at the MTC within a few days, and my source of connection, support, and relief was gone. My world became unsettling as I moved into my dorm, met new hall mates, and familiarized myself with the layout of the campus. I knew my brother still loved me, but he was not there to comfort me. It was a hollow experience. I felt numb when I thought about him and was consumed with sadness. Fortunately, I was blessed with plenty of distractions in my new surroundings. As the months went on, I leaned on new people and found comfort in my previously unfamiliar environment.

I would venture to say that similar to the pain of not being able to be with my brother, not being able to feel God's love and Spirit has been my most emotionally painful experience. It has hurt my heart so often and filled me with anger, confusion, betrayal, and mistrust. The fluctuation between being able to feel His Spirit followed by such a heavy void has been torture.

It can feel as if I am merely going through the motions without reward. It can cause me to doubt past experiences I've had with the Spirit. I used to find myself wondering if others were faking their testimonies. After all, I would be doing the same spiritual stuff they were, but I was not getting the same results.

It seems like God should show up the most in our darkest moments of depression and anxiety. He should be bringing us light right then. It seems cruel that He would leave us feeling so dark. Why would an all-loving God do something like that? It's hard to make sense of it.

The pain I felt when my brother left was rough. I knew he had not abandoned me, yet I also knew I wasn't allowed to reach out to him. I did try to sneak into the MTC once with my cousin, but they wouldn't let me see him. Their security van followed us out. Whoops.

Still, I knew my brother loved me and would be there for me if he could. God is the same. He loves us. I'm not sure exactly why we can't feel the Spirit when we are struggling with depression or anxiety, but I know the Lord wants to be there for us—and even though it feels lonely, we are not alone. At the October 2020 general conference, Elder Dieter F. Uchtdorf said,

> In a way, we are seeds. And for seeds to reach their potential, they must be buried before they can sprout. It is my witness that though at times we may feel buried by the trials of life or surrounded by emotional darkness, the love of God and the blessings of the restored gospel of Jesus Christ will bring something unimaginable to spring forth. . . .
>
> We all must walk through difficult times, for it is in these times of adversity that we learn principles that fortify our characters and cause us to draw closer to God. . . . our Heavenly Father knows that we suffer, and because we are His children, He will not abandon us. God will watch over and shepherd you during these times of uncertainty and fear. He knows you. He hears your pleas. He is faithful and dependable. He will fulfill His promises.

We may currently feel as if we are being buried, just as a seed is buried. Elder Uchtdorf's beautiful promise of "something unimaginable" gives us the hope and encouragement we need to press on. Though they're not something I ever enjoy, I do know that trials teach us a great deal. Having hope or

light at the end of the tunnel motivates us to keep going and to progress.

—

As I search for yellow, the peace I find in God is sweet. My journey of searching for yellow has created a powerful connection with and understanding of Him. I have learned through repeated experiences that He is there even when I can't feel Him. The way I talk with Him now is different from before. I have become more real and open. When I can't feel Him, I tell Him.

I hope differently. While in my darkest moments, even when I don't feel hope, I can believe hope is there. Even when I don't feel loved, I can believe I am loved. And that's just enough to keep me going and pushing forward.

Though I can't always feel His Spirit, He is always right beside me, encouraging me and pushing me to search for my yellow. Now that I understand He is always there, I search for yellow differently. I watch for Him in ways I never used to, and I am able to see Him where I didn't see Him before.

—

Despite the pain that has come from feeling abandoned, I can honestly say that depression and anxiety and searching for yellow have given me a greater insight and appreciation for God. Though I am far from understanding the great and powerful things He does, I feel His all-knowing and all-loving purpose. I know He has not abandoned us. Below, you'll find my charts detailing my ability to feel Him near during the various stages of depression and anxiety.

Feeling His Spirit
Depression

Mild	I am able to feel God's love often. I recognize the Spirit in my life and feel the peace it brings. Sometimes I am overcome with peaceful thoughts or feelings.
Moderate	I am sometimes able to feel God's love, recognize the Spirit in my life, and feel the peace the Spirit brings. At times, I can be overcome with peaceful thoughts or feelings even though I may revert to depressed emotions almost immediately.
Severe	I have a hard time feeling God's love, which leads to feelings of unworthiness. Feeling the Spirit becomes somewhat more of a chore. I rarely feel His Spirit. Frustration with God and/or myself sets in. However, as I have experienced growth over the years, I am able to be more patient with God. I have learned He is there even when I don't feel Him.
Suicidal	I am desperate to feel God's love. I do not feel any peace. I can't feel the Spirit. Feelings of complete abandonment and loneliness envelop me. I become nonemotional or angry with God and others.
Numb	I don't feel God's love which may turn into anger.

Feeling His Spirit
Anxiety

Mild	I am able to feel God's love most of the time. I feel as if I can connect with the Lord and feel His Spirit when I try.

(continued on next page)

Moderate	Moments of feeling the Spirit can keep me going, but not feeling the Spirit for a prolonged time can deepen the anxiety. I feel as if I am "grasping" to feel the Spirit and God's love.
Severe	There is an intense struggle to find hope and connection with the Lord. Feeling the Spirit seems impossible. I don't feel like the Lord answers my prayers, and I experience painful loneliness.
Panic Attack	I used to think it was the end. After being here multiple times, I am able to remind myself that it is temporary. I call out to the Lord more often for strength, even though I can't feel the Spirit.
Anxiety Fog	I can't feel the Spirit. I feel spiritually numb.

Chapter 25

A Choice Had To Be Made

Staying Spiritually Strong

As I realized there was a connection between my depression and anxiety and my inability to feel the Spirit, I knew I had to make a decision. Though I have been given this trial and can't remove it from my life, I have found certain things that can change my experiences and outlook.

I became intrigued by the seemingly mixed signals of feeling and not feeling the Spirit. It didn't seem to make sense. My feelings of abandonment and anger left me feeling like leaving God altogether. However, I had grown to love Him and the gospel, and I couldn't deny the experiences I had. So I simply assumed my issues were to blame. It seemed obvious there were plenty of things I needed to fix about myself.

That's when I noticed my kids struggling. They felt God's Spirit, then almost immediately felt abandoned. Their goodness and light were so clear and obvious. Why would they feel stripped of feeling God's love almost instantaneously?

I wanted to dig deeper and learn more for my kids' sake. What was this confusion that seemed to be given directly from the Lord? My kids are good and kind and have a great desire to follow the Lord. Why would the Lord abandon them? It didn't add up. Maybe, just maybe, He hadn't abandoned us. Maybe this was an actual part of the hellish trial we were given.

———

Believing that He does not leave us has been a driving force behind my motivation to find relief and comfort. In the 2001 October general conference, Elder Joseph B. Wirthlin said, "Though you may feel weary, though you sometimes may not be able to see the way, know that your Father in Heaven will never forsake His righteous followers. He will not leave you comfortless. He will be at your side, yes, guiding you every step of the way."

As I have taken the approach that He has not abandoned us, my life has utterly changed. Let me be clear: there was *not* some immediate revelation and then everything was dandy. Unfortunately, that's rarely if ever the case with these things. Trust me, I hear you. It's a pain in the rear, and like everyone else, I wish it wasn't such a long, grueling process. But the more I insisted I could instantaneously get better, the more I hindered my progress. The yellow was limited and sparse.

Still, even though it has taken time and learning, I am able to feel and recognize His spirit more. I feel abandoned less often. My hope is stronger and more reassuring. My testimony of His love and concern for me is greater than ever before.

Here's what I know:

- · I enjoy feeling close to the Lord.
- · I don't feel the Spirit when I am severely depressed.
- · I can't feel the Spirit when I have severe anxiety.
- · I miss the Spirit when I can't feel it.

- I enjoy the guidance and comfort of the Spirit.
- I want to feel the Spirit as often as possible.
- I want to feel like I am pleasing the Lord.

In order to change my outlook, I had to stop assuming that

- I was failing, unworthy, or doing something wrong.
- When I couldn't feel the Spirit, it meant He left me.
- When I couldn't feel the Spirit, it meant He didn't love me.
- Struggling with depression and anxiety made me less of a person.
- There was no hope.

In order to change my outlook, I had to understand that

- Understanding myself is up to me.
- Pushing myself and progressing is up to me.
- Staying spiritually strong is a choice.
- No one can force me to stay spiritually strong.
- Hope can be there even if I don't feel it.
- God's love and Spirit can be there even if I don't feel them.

The following two charts detail my feelings regarding spiritual strength at the different levels of depression and anxiety. See if you can relate to some of them.

Staying Spiritually Strong
Depression

Mild	I'm usually able to do the "typical" things that connect me to His Spirit. I recognize that doing something good or righteous does not mean instantly feeling the Spirit. It's less of a chore to try to feel His presence.
Moderate	I must keep moving and strive to be close to Heavenly Father. I lose spiritual connection easily, but I can catch glimpses of peace, and I try to focus on those moments.
Severe	I must focus on truth: truth about myself, truth about God, truth about what others see in me. The more truth I allow myself to see, the better. I must rely on past spiritual experiences. I used to think the Lord had abandoned me. I have now experienced this cycle enough to know that even when I can't feel Him, the Lord does not leave me.
Suicidal	I'm honestly not sure how I stay spiritually strong while suicidal other than make the best decisions I can for the situation I am in and hope for mercy from the Lord. My situation becomes less about "staying spiritually strong" and more about emotional and physical survival.
Numb	Feeling numb is like hitting a dead end. It creates a sense of hopelessness. But as I look back on past experiences, I am more able to have faith that this will pass. I can see the cycle and know I will be able to feel His Spirit again. Although my mind tells me I am spiritually damned, I have decided to fight against believing it. I remind myself that God loves me even when I can't feel His love.

Staying Spiritually Strong
Anxiety

Mild	I may feel comforted through the "typical" things that connect me to His Spirit. I can "soak up" things such as conference talks, etc.

(continued on next page)

Moderate   It is difficult to do the "typical" things that connect me to His Spirit. These cause more anxiety than relaxation. Feeling the Spirit is unusual.

Severe   Can't feel the Spirit through "typical" gospel things. I rely on the hope of feeling the Spirit again once I am able to relieve the anxiety. I can feel comforted and recognize the Spirit through others with whom I feel emotionally safe.

Panic Attack   I am mostly inside my head at this point. There is a lot of talking to God but not feeling Him. To stay spiritually strong, I rely on past experiences with Him. I have cycled enough throughout my life that I know it is temporary (even though I can't see or feel it at this point) and I will be able to feel the Spirit once I get into a healthier place emotionally.

Anxiety Fog   It is frustrating to try to feel the Spirit, but I get glimpses of it. I get frustrated with myself and the mental blocks that get in the way of feeling the Spirit, but I rely on previously experienced faith-building experiences.

Chapter 26

Tick, Tick, Tick

Possible Triggers to Get to This Point

MY HUSBAND AND I were signed up to do one of those self-reliance sessions. You know, the ones held in the ward for multiple weeks in a row. The one we signed up for was about finances and how to use money wisely. Yay.

My family didn't have much money when I was growing up so, you guessed it, the class itself was a trigger. And it didn't end there. The classes started just as COVID struck, so stress was at an all-time high. Another trigger. There's more: my husband's office was closed due to COVID, so he wasn't working. Yet another trigger.

With all those triggers, I struggled terribly through the initial class. It took every ounce of courage for me to stay through the Zoom meeting and periodically show my half-smiling face on the screen.

As soon as the meeting was over, I disappeared. I went to my room, where I collapsed, physically and emotionally. I knew it was coming, and I tried to fight it, but it kicked into a full-blown panic attack. Needless to say, my husband and I pulled out of the rest of the sessions.

I watch for triggers but don't always recognize or catch them in time. I shouldn't beat myself up, though sometimes I still do. Elder Joseph B. Wirthlin comforts us by saying,

> I take the steps that I can take. Even with the limitations of age, I can still take one step at a time. To do what I can is all my Heavenly Father now requires of me. And it is all He requires of you, regardless of your disabilities, limitations, or insecurities. We don't have to be perfect today. We don't have to be better than someone else. All we have to do is to be the very best we can.

The focus should not be on how many steps we are able to take. Instead, it should be about the direction we are going. The Lord wants us to reach for Him no matter what trials seem to consume us.

Sifting through our thoughts and figuring out where they come from can bring a natural awareness of our triggers. We can use this knowledge to develop the power to change. Though I initially felt guilty that I wasn't "strong enough" to complete the self-reliance class, I soon felt peace and reassured that Heavenly Father knew my limits. He knows me, understands my triggers, and recognizes when I am pushing to do what I can.

Notice in the charts below the triggers that can often lead to certain levels of depression and anxiety for me. Do you have similar triggers?

Possible Triggers to Get to This Point
Depression

Mild	This can simply be a reaction to daily challenges.
Moderate	This can be from the way others treat me. It also can be from my interpretation of what's happening around me. My mind can be my biggest enemy. In addition, it becomes a problem when I have too little time to regroup or too many hard things coming at me all at once.
Severe	This is sometimes an after-effect of something big or dramatic that just happened. Prolonged sickness can be a problem. Not caring for myself in times of moderate depression can be a problem. A recent severe drop in mood will increase the chance of another until I am able to experience a significant period of emotional regularity.
Suicidal	This is typically due to not being aware of my needs or not taking care of myself while in severe depression.
Numb	This can stem from dealing with either prolonged depression or too many hard things coming at me all at once.

Possible Triggers to Get to This Point
Anxiety

Mild	This can simply be a reaction to my daily challenges. Also, trying to get out of depression can cause anxiety.
Moderate	This comes from feeling a loss of control over my surroundings, feeling stupid, reading or watching intense media, the way others treat me, my interpretation of what is happening around me, too little time to regroup, or too many hard things coming at me all at once.

(continued on next page)

Severe	This is sometimes an aftereffect of something big or dramatic that just happened in my life. Not caring for myself in times of moderate anxiety can cause problems. A recent severe episode with anxiety will increase the chance of another until I am able to experience a significant period of emotional regularity.
Panic Attack	This can come on gradually or suddenly. It can also be caused by having to do something difficult, not attending to severe anxiety, and as a result of negative past experiences.
Anxiety Fog	This can occur as a result of conversations where I remember something from the past or other stressful topics. It can also be caused by being with others who treat me condescendingly. Having anxiety in general brings on the anxiety fog.

Chapter 27

It's Gonna Be a Surprise

What May Help

Sometimes I get crazy ideas. My husband came home from work one day to find me slapping drywall mud onto a focal wall in our family room. Did I have experience with drywall mud? Nope. Did I care? Nope.

I think my husband almost had his own panic attack. He asked what I was doing, and I'm pretty sure I said something like, "I'm not sure yet." I figured it would be a surprise to both of us. That probably didn't reassure him.

Once the drywall was on, I painted it. Then I smeared more drywall splotches on the wall. Because why not? Rather than brushing additional coats of paint in a consistent manner,

I did so randomly. I added browns, oranges, and golds. I'm sure it was totally cool at the time.

Every day for about a week, the wall looked different when my husband came home. Looking back, I wonder if he thought I'd lost it. I acknowledged that the wall was pretty wild, but I soaked in the experience and had fun with it. It became a focal point of our home. Not like there was a choice!

When it was time to sell our house, we got a little concerned. Who in the world would buy a house with this randomly designed wall? But, thankfully, we found a lucky buyer. Ironically, the wall was a solid selling point. They loved it!

Though I haven't recently done anything with drywall mud, I've found I love to create. I love the process and feeling of accomplishment it brings. I love the mental escape. It's relaxing and healing. I am motivated by the before and relish in the excitement of the after.

When we're depressed, it can help us to be creative or find something to look forward to. Especially when the depression is severe, we may need something to persuade us to get out of bed. This can be as simple as an enticing breakfast shake, lighting a candle, or running an errand.

Anxiety forces us to streamline our schedules and make sure we are balancing our needs because panic can set in even with the simplest of tasks. We can spread out the tasks, such as going to the bank or making a phone call, that make us anxious. Or we might find that condensing tasks and getting them over with quickly helps. Monitoring ourselves to see what works best can aid in preventing emotional lows or escalations in anxiety.

Making commitments we can keep strengthens us both physically and emotionally. Thinking outside of the box not only keeps us moving forward, it stirs and wakes our foggy brains.

While experiencing depression and anxiety, we may find things that help and others that don't. One thing that's helped me maintain emotional balance is to keep a quick-reference list of the reasons I might experience depression drops or anxiety spikes.

In monitoring my depression drops, I have discovered a few basic triggers that make things worsen very quickly:

- Illness/allergy season
- Social media
- Hunger
- Upsetting someone
- Feeling as if I am failing in multiple aspects of my life (wife, mom, gospel, etc.)
- Feeling stupid

Things that can make my anxiety spike include:

- Confrontation/anger
- A huge to-do list
- Clutter
- Upsetting someone
- Feeling as if I am failing in multiple aspects of my life (wife, mom, gospel, and so on)
- Going to the store/church/social gatherings/temple

During a drop or spike, I can refer to my list to see if there is an explanation for what I'm feeling. I can then assess my immediate needs and begin working to stabilize my emotions.

In addition to this list, consider drafting a more specific list. Be careful, though, as your list grows, that it doesn't become overwhelming and tempt you to simply avoid everything on it as this undermines your potential for growth. I have found therapy to be specifically helpful with facing my list head-on instead of avoiding certain aspects of life.

Learning what heals us is a continual process. While in a healthier frame of mind, we may find it beneficial to collect a list of past experiences. When possible, we can plan ahead and create lists of the things that help. Our lists will change over time, but that is perfect. Ideally, we will be changing too.

Determining what can help us heal while we are struggling can sometimes be difficult. It may cause aggravation and disappointment. When we are in the middle of the muck, we can begin with trying an assorted number of things that are healthy and bring us close to Christ. Though we may feel hopeless, we can dig deep, push ourselves, and identify what helps us find yellow. And when we find that pinch of reprieve, that smidgen of yellow, it's glorious. The following are the things I've discovered that help me push through the depression and anxiety:

What May Help
Depression

Mild	Putting myself in an uplifting environment. Inviting people over who know me and uplift me. Serving others. Getting out of my head and making sure I'm taking care of myself. Signing up for service on a future date, which gives me time to prepare emotionally and physically. When I serve, it forces me to get out of the house. Doing projects and baking are big go-to activities for me. Lighting candles and enjoying fresh air helps. Getting out of the house is a must. Connecting with nature through things such as casual bike riding, swimming, weeding, washing off the patio, or reading a book outside.

(continued on next page)

Moderate Making sure I am having "me time" in moderation; too much or too little can make things worse. I need to set and accomplish realistic goals each day. Avoiding beating myself up for not being like "everyone else" is crucial. I must allow myself to recognize the good I do each day. I need to stay aware of situations, conversations, and environments (triggers) that add to the risk of dropping further.

Severe I must have a complete awareness of my mind and body. This includes staying aware of situations, conversations, and environments I can't handle. Removing myself from emotionally damaging situations helps, as do positive brain repetitions. I need to allow myself to cry, feel down, feel angry, sleep, and believe there is hope even when I don't feel it. I must remind myself this is a phase.

Suicidal Just as with severe depression, I must have a complete awareness of my mind and body. This includes staying aware of situations, conversations, and environments I can't handle. Removing myself from emotionally damaging situations helps, as do positive brain repetitions. I need to allow myself to cry, feel down, feel angry, sleep, and believe there is hope even when I don't feel it. I must remind myself this is a phase.

Numb The numbness is a defense mechanism. In order to break the cycle, I must deal with the issues at hand.

What May Help
Anxiety

Mild	I enjoy doing wood, paint, and design projects. Remodeling homes and creating beautiful spaces is one of my passions. I love sharing hope, especially with the youth. Being with my children and reading books or watching movies with them often brings me peace and comfort. Good, clean, cheesy chick flicks are right up my alley. I love feeling the Spirit and relish it when I am able. I love prayer and the rawness of talking to my Heavenly Father about my blessings, needs, desires, and worries. At this point, I am able to create larger goals.
Moderate	As I work on being creative, such as with wood projects, I feel a sense of accomplishment as well as enjoy quiet, pondering time. Goals will typically be things that are a few days out. For example, I may volunteer to bring food to an activity the following week, or I may invite a child's friend over for the next day.
Severe	With severe anxiety, I might need to sit or lie down. I must separate myself from others and leave any social environments. I use breathing, body-relaxing techniques, and brain repetition to calm my body and mind. I clench my muscles and then relax them. Sucking on sour candy or chewing on ice shocks my system. I crave my husband's hugs, as they create a sense of safety. I remind myself that this is a phase.
Panic Attack	The immediate need is for me to lie down. I must separate myself from other people and leave any kind of social environment. Often, I need to take medication to help me relax and fall asleep. I hide in the shower so I can freely cry and release my emotions.
Anxiety Fog	Mental blocks create an instant feeling of stupidity, so I prefer to leave the situation or environment. I may shower so I can cry freely. I pray often and wait to feel His calmness.

Chapter 28

Potato Potaaaaahtoe

What Does Not Help

My neighbor and I were close friends for years. He came over all the time and hung out with me and my brothers. On one occasion, he told me about some chocolate-covered noodles he had just eaten. They sounded glorious and super easy to make. I decided to surprise my family and make some before they came home.

I cooked the noodles until they were perfect, then melted chocolate and poured it over the cooled noodles. Something didn't seem right, but I couldn't pinpoint what.

About that time, my mom came home. Looking a bit confused, she asked what I was doing. I told her about the chocolate-covered noodles the neighbor made. She smiled and explained that the type of noodles he was referring to was the crunchy Chinese type. He wasn't talking about your good ol' spaghetti noodles. Potato, potaaaaahhtoe. Did it really matter the type of noodle I was using?

Apparently, it did. This explained the runny, wet noodle mess in front of me. I wasn't using the right type of noodle.

Not sure why my neighbor was so rude as to not tell me about this important detail. It obviously had nothing to do with *my* noodle knowledge.

I'm pretty sure we dumped the mess out. We ate some pretty creative things growing up, but this one was unsalvageable. But isn't it through experimenting with different ideas that we figure out what works and what doesn't?

As we search for things that help with our depression and anxiety, we will come across things that do not help. For example, I can experience very sharp drops in mood while scrolling through social media. Obviously, social media has plenty of uplifting sites and posts, but I can drop even then. I need to have a purpose when I view social media. I quickly find what I am looking for, carefully monitor my thoughts, and then get off as quickly as I can. Another example is shopping. Especially when depressed, it doesn't make sense for me to aimlessly search Amazon. Having a purpose keeps me focused and in better control of the decisions I make.

Though it's possible that hearing stories about others' struggles can be helpful, it doesn't bring relief for me. When I am in an emotionally dark place, I am unable to process others' stories. That may sound selfish, but it's simply survival.

Granted, others' stories can provide important insights and help us understand we are not alone. However, in hearing stories or seeing social media posts, I often find myself comparing my struggles with theirs. I begin to assume that for me to find relief, my "recovery" story must look like theirs. This aggravates my feelings of failure and only makes things worse. Forcing myself to have identical experiences to someone else typically accelerates my downward spiral. Instead, I find it helps to dive into a search for what helps *me*.

I must keep a balance by being aware of what I am choosing to do. I must pay attention not only to how I am spending my time but what emotions are surfacing and why. This may sound exhausting, but it is extremely helpful in the long run.

Testing recipes helps us learn what does and does not work—and that includes recipes for relieving depression and anxiety. There will be times when we find new and exciting recipes that work well. But there are times when we use recipes or strategies that do not help. Our recipe can become a hot mess in front of us, and we may need to start over. And that's okay! Check out the following list of the things that do not help me when I'm struggling, and see if perhaps you can identify with any of them.

What Does Not Help
Depression

Mild	Others treating me as if I am exaggerating is painful. It's not helpful for those who know my struggle to bring it up every time they see me. Experiences that make me feel as if I am stupid or not of worth worsen the drop. Social media posts, positive and negative, can cause a drop.
Moderate	Allowing myself to believe negative thoughts perpetuates the drop. I am experiencing feelings of "failure" in multiple areas of my life, and the more I think about it, the worse it can get.

(continued on next page)

Severe	It does not help to be around people who tell me to get over it or just be happy. Listening to someone tell stories of their friends who have suffered and how they got past it is also not helpful. It doesn't help to have people avoid me because they know I am struggling. I'm not helped by others watching me as if they're thinking *Is she okay today?*
Suicidal	Hibernating makes things worse but becomes part of the vicious cycle since facing the world feels impossible.
Numb	Sleeping too much makes it harder to have any motivation and causes me to stay inside my head. Being with others who have harsh personalities creates a sense of emotionally caving.

What Does Not Help
Anxiety

Mild	Having a lot on my to-do list or a cluttered home raises my anxiety. If multiple family members are having a bad day, I often feel responsible and take on the emotional stress.
Moderate	Any intense or even slightly intense situation or experience is not helpful. Things like movies, books, and conversations that cause even a temporary rise in emotions can result in severe anxiety.
Severe	Conversations that result in me feeling as if I am failing are unhelpful. Not taking time to let myself breathe and work through my emotions increases my anxiety. Being with others I don't feel understand me makes it worse.
Panic Attack	It's not helpful to be with those I am not close to. Being in a public situation where I can't release my emotions is very difficult.
Anxiety Fog	Being around people or situations that add to my insecurities or make me feel stupid is not helpful at all.

Chapter 29

The Mangled Response

Reaction to Others

FOR SOME REASON, I've accumulated a handful of random clipboards over the years. I've clung to this small collection just in case someone suddenly needs a clipboard, I guess.

When my daughter was young, she loved crafts. One day, she snuck into my oh-so-important clipboard stash and began crafting. Eventually, with a smile on her face, she presented me a clipboard covered with random pieces of scrapbook paper she had glued all over it.

A healthy, normal reaction to such a sweet gesture may have been, "Thank you." But not me. Nope. I didn't react well. I began to chew her out while sobbing, a completely unrealistic reaction. It took me five or ten minutes to snap out of my appalling tantrum. I apologized to my daughter and vowed in my heart to do better. This was a massive clue that I wasn't doing so hot emotionally at the time.

I still have that clipboard and have since sealed her design on the back with Mod-Podge glue. It serves as a reminder of the good and bad of that moment. Ironically, when she tenderly decorated it, she intentionally tore paper and designed the pieces to lie in a random pattern. The torn paper glued onto the board feels symbolic of that moment, that day.

———

One of the worst feelings for me is knowing I've overreacted or been unkind. I hate when others suffer because of my mood swings. Though I know that tender, unconditional love typically helps me the most, it's not fair for me to expect reactions specifically fitted to my needs. I must allow those around me to have ups and downs too. Paying attention to where I am emotionally, including watching my reactions closer and catching them early, helps prevent stronger reactions than I intend, something that benefits everyone involved.

In addition, the more I communicate, the better. It has been helpful for me to share with others what I am feeling and what I need. This allows others to understand what is happening. All the while, I make sure I am caring for those around me and not just focusing on myself. This creates space for me to openly acknowledge that I am struggling and to take ownership of my reactions.

Obviously, the goal is not perfection, even though that would be nice. The goal is to do the best we can while continually assessing and apologizing when we make mistakes. Communication widens my awareness of how I am reacting and provides an opportunity for me to react in healthier, more loving ways. See if you can relate to any of the descriptions in the charts on the next page.

Reaction to Others
Depression

Mild	I can usually make it through the day without others noticing that I'm depressed. It's fairly easy to control my words and actions.
Moderate	I feel on and off and that it's hard to stay in one place emotionally. There are lots of ups and downs. I experience quick, smaller highs and quick though manageable drops.
Severe	I become more impatient and snappy. I also become reclusive and avoid social settings.
Suicidal	I become more impatient and uncaring. I also become reclusive and avoid social settings.
Numb	I pull away from those around me. I am snippy and may come across as uncaring.

Reaction to Others
Anxiety

Mild	I can usually make it through the day without others noticing that I have anxiety. It's fairly easy to control my words and actions.
Moderate	I teeter between irritability and feeling as if I am in control of my emotions.
Severe	I feel tense, jumpy, and irritable. I can get snippy and yell about things that don't make sense to yell about.
Panic Attack	I react out of fear. I try to go somewhere where others won't see me.
Anxiety Fog	I come across as shocked and confused. I quickly become sharp with my words.

Chapter 30

I Need! I Need!

Personal Neediness

MY FRIEND KATHY refuses to be needy. She's one of those rock stars who has no clue she's a rock star. It's pretty fabulous. It's almost comical to see her run around and create magic all the while thinking she's an average human being. Nope. Not the case. She will break her back before asking for help. One day, I think God decided He wanted to teach her a little lesson.

She and her family were moving from Texas to Arizona. They had piled two moving trucks to the brim with their belongings. One truck held the main portion of their home, and a smaller truck included items from their garage and yard.

Both trucks were loaded and ready to go. One more quick stop and they would be off to Arizona. As her husband drove to pick up the tow hitch, the engine in the large moving truck suddenly began to smoke. He saw fire under the hood and immediately jumped out of the truck. He stood on the side of the road and watched as the truck rapidly burned all their belongings.

I received notification through an email that their family was moving into our ward within twenty-four hours and barely had anything to their name. The ward rallied around them and provided the immediate necessities. I kept hearing that Kathy claimed they were fine and didn't need anything.

Say what?

They had lost everything from their home. But once I got to know Kathy, her comment made sense. I found that she is strong, kind, and typically one to refuse help. She is used to being on the giving end.

I have been blessed to know Kathy over the years. I admire her strength and awareness. She consistently strives to create a better environment for herself as well as those around her. She still doesn't like to ask for help, but she has a new outlook. She understands that sometimes, whether we like it or not, we actually need help. And that's okay.

———

I'm not sure why people are so confused by my emotional roller coaster. I make sense to myself all the time. I either need lots of help, no help, tons of attention, to be left alone, or somewhere in between. People should be able to read my mind and assess what I need, even before I can. How difficult is that?

Personal Neediness
Depression

Mild	I feel fairly strong and independent. I am usually able to clearly understand my needs.

(continued on next page)

Moderate   I am more emotionally needy and crave extra reassurance. I become confused as to where I stand in other people's hearts. I need extra communication and touch.

Severe   I become emotionally paranoid and experience panicky feelings of insecurity. I desperately look to those I am close to for strength. Other times, I feel numb and pull away from everyone around me. I begin to feel like giving up and don't want to need others in my life.

Suicidal   I physically and emotionally pull away from everyone. I begin to believe I "can't" need anyone anymore because I simply make others' lives worse.

Numb   It feels like I don't need anyone, but after experiencing this over and over, I have realized that a more accurate statement would be that I don't *want* to need anyone.

Personal Neediness
Anxiety

Mild   I feel fairly strong and independent. I'm usually able to clearly understand my needs.

Moderate   I yearn to be close, then pull away from others, which gives them confusing signals. I need lots of reassurance and love, including comforting words and physical touch.

Severe   I push away from others because I feel as if I'm being attacked. I need lots of reassurance and love, including comforting words and physical touch.

Panic Attack I'm overwhelmed with fear. I like space and don't want anyone around to see me like this.

Anxiety Fog I pull away from others to avoid feeling humiliated or embarrassed.

Chapter 31

The Connection of a Friend

Friendships

A COUPLE OF years ago, I was having lunch with my friend Nicole. During our lunch, I mentioned my struggle with depression and anxiety. She told me that was not something she personally struggled with but asked if I would tell her more.

As I shared some of my experiences, I remember her looking closely at me and saying, "I can't imagine how difficult that must be." It hit me that she was right. It *is* difficult. It's painful, embarrassing, frustrating, and lonely. I appreciated her insight, kindness, and concern.

Since then, Nicole and I have talked about gobs of other things. Every once in a while, she asks how I am doing, and her concern is always real. It's refreshing. I feel important. I feel loved and validated. I feel comfortable having a fun time and comfortable having a hard time. There's never judgment.

Depression and anxiety force us to focus on ourselves, something that cramps my style. I don't want everything to be about me. I want to constantly give, serve, and love. But I have no choice. I need to work on healing myself while desperately searching for yellow. Once I feel somewhat normal again, I get excited. Why? It means I can now be the yellow for someone else. See the charts below of what I experience with friendships during various stages of depression and anxiety.

Friendships
Depression

Mild	I'm able to be in a variety of positive or negative situations, including being with others who are unkind or don't know me well. My resilience is somewhat strong, and I can introduce myself, speak up in church, have a party, and so on.
Moderate	I enjoy being with close friends who help me feel emotionally safe, loved, and secure. I'm comfortable being myself and expressing what I'm experiencing. I may also carefully weigh who I can see and when, depending on how I am doing.
Severe	I have a strong need to get away from others. I assume that if others saw my "true" self, they wouldn't like me. My emotions are typically too deep and dark for me to feel comfortable being around others. On the other hand, it can be a good time for me to invite those I am very close to over to my home; they help me feel an emotional lift and support.
Suicidal	I don't want to be with friends because they may sense I am struggling, and I don't want them to see the dark truth.
Numb	I typically want distance from others to avoid them seeing me in a noncaring mood. I may be quite sarcastic.

Friendships

Anxiety

Mild Though it makes me a bit nervous for friends to see me uptight, I can usually cover it pretty well at this point.

Moderate It takes a bit more effort to be with friends as I feel quite anxious and afraid I will not only make mistakes but come across as rude or hurtful.

Severe I don't like being with friends since I know I am acting a bit more irrational and I don't want them to see my "weaknesses."

Panic Attack I have no contact with friends at this point. I am definitely in "hibernation mode."

Anxiety Fog When my mind is in a fog, I have learned to speak less during conversations. I rely on comfort and lack of judgment from friends as I push through.

Chapter 32

Out on the Town

Social Situations

During a Relief Society activity, we were asked to bring one of our favorite things. The purpose was to share something we loved with the other sisters in the room. This way, they could get to know us better. Sisters brought blankets and soaps, photos of grandchildren, and letters from loved ones.

I brought a long strip of reclaimed wood that had red paint worn off one of the sides. The wood happened to be about three feet long, but I couldn't bear the thought of cutting it into a smaller piece for the activity. So there I went, marching into the activity with a big ol' piece of wood.

I began to feel a bit self-conscious. The wood itself wasn't from something special, like my grandpa's barn. It was simply a leftover piece of wood I had bought for a project I had worked on. I just love old wood. When it was my turn to explain, I felt lame. The wood wasn't sentimental, nor was it valuable.

Granted, I didn't look at it as any ol' piece of wood. It was a piece that had been reclaimed from a barn somewhere in the Midwest. To me, it had character and a story behind it. It was beautiful and reminded me of the old buildings and homes I saw while growing up in the East. Yet I still felt ridiculous. I felt as if everyone around me was confused and silently laughing at my contribution.

Quite awhile later, I received a text from my friend Pam with a picture of an old, beautiful barn. Pam was on a trip to the East, and she had thought of me when driving past this barn.

It was then I realized that my contribution to the Relief Society activity wasn't ridiculous after all. Maybe, just maybe, the judgment I felt in that social situation was actually due to a lack of self-confidence. I had been surrounded by women who loved me. But because of the anxiety I felt, I had limited what I might have gained that evening.

Attending social events is still quite challenging. Sometimes I can go; sometimes I can't. However, when I can go, I try to pay attention. I watch for truth and goodness. I soak up time with those who love me unconditionally. I remind myself that true friends, even if they don't see the beauty of the wood itself, are willing to appreciate the wood's beauty with me. Check out my lists for social situations.

Social Situations
Depression

Mild   I am interested in social situations and enjoy the encouragement and support of others. I am able to be around various groups of people—those I deem "emotionally safe" as well as those who are "emotionally unsafe." I am open to talking with others about my struggles while still feeling fairly secure with who I am.

Moderate   Although I can still be myself with others, social situations are a struggle. Holding a conversation may be more difficult, and there will often be a depression drop once I am home.

Severe   I typically avoid all social situations. I experience extreme sensitivity to situations and events around me.

Suicidal   When attending social situations, I watch for reasons why everyone would be better off without me.

Numb   I can attend social situations but may care little about what is happening around me. I feel little to no excitement, sadness, etc.

Social Situations
Anxiety

Mild   I am a bit more sensitive during social activities. But I can talk myself into going to activities, and they often end up being a nice, needed relief.

Moderate   It's more difficult to get out the door and attend social events. It is a gamble as to whether the event will relax me or heighten my anxiety.

Severe   Going to events is extremely difficult since my anxiety is so consuming. If I must go, I avoid eye contact and conversations. I might need to take bathroom breaks to stay on top of the anxiety and not go into a panic attack. I avoid phone calls and texts. I go into "hibernation mode."

Panic Attack   I remove myself from social settings as I feel a panic attack coming on.

Anxiety Fog   I can attend social settings but feel really stupid because I can't think straight. I typically stay quiet and observe rather than join conversations.

Chapter 33

Jump on It

Motivation

I GUESS SOME people are altogether naturally motivated. They can just go and get things done. I think naturally motivated people are annoying. Okay, okay . . . not annoying, just intimidating. Reeeeeeeally intimidating. For me, it can be impossible to stay motivated while fighting the heaviness of depression and anxiety.

Something as simple as watching an intense movie can kick my anxiety into high gear and leave me feeling on edge for days. Though I may be able to keep up physically, I am emotionally uptight and snippy. I feel attacked, though there is no threat. Eventually, after frantically searching for yellow while battling such high emotions, I can get to a healthier, calmer state.

When living with depression and anxiety, it's common to experience frequent emotional interruptions. Though we can learn to take certain precautions, there's no way to *always* know when we will get hit. These interruptions throw off our motivation and can greatly affect our ability to accomplish anything.

There's a difference between being motivated and happy yippee-skippy about what we're trying to do. Happy yippee-skippy is definitely more difficult to pull off. However, once we discover what truly motivates us, we find we are given additional strength to accomplish what matters most.

We can't wait for motivation to be consistent. Instead, we must watch for the bits of motivation that pop up here and there and take advantage of them. The charts below include descriptions of how motivated I feel in different degrees of depression and anxiety. Can you relate?

Motivation
Depression

Mild	I feel strong enough to get up and move.
Moderate	I find myself trying to do things (like too much time on the TV, etc.) to avoid depressive emotions. I set manageable goals to get through each day and feel accomplishment.
Severe	I get things done out of sheer responsibility, embarrassment, or emotional force. I take baby steps to allow myself a sense of accomplishment and forward movement.
Suicidal	Just like severe depression, I get things done either out of sheer responsibility, embarrassment, or emotional force. It is more difficult to set any goals since I feel useless.
Numb	I don't care about getting things done. More than likely, I will avoid the to-do list right in front of me.

Motivation
Anxiety

Mild	My confidence is mild but present. My confidence strengthens with accomplishing goals and feeling peace and love from the Lord.

(continued on next page)

Moderate   It can be a struggle to accomplish things, but I am usually able to push forward. I try to keep my confidence up by accomplishing daily goals and asking the Lord for help.

Severe   I feel deep panic over even the tiniest of things. I have little to no confidence and am sure I will mess anything and everything up. I feel like a failure.

Panic Attack   I can't focus on anything besides getting through these panicked thoughts and feelings.

Anxiety Fog   It can be a struggle to accomplish things, but I am usually able to push forward. I have to break down and simplify any tasks at hand.

Chapter 34

Mind + Body = Chaos

Physical

WHILE I ENJOY the peacefulness of the library and discovering books I've never read, my family and I go through phases of visiting the library. Sometimes we visit multiple times a week; other times we may not visit for months.

One day while at the library, I saw a man happily carrying a three- or four-year-old on his shoulders. I thought it was a bit strange for him to be carrying a child on his shoulders while in a library. It caught me off guard, so I watched closer.

I was instantly taken aback when I realized the man had no arms. My mind whirled, and I began to see the experience in a different light. Not only was this dad at the library with his child, he was showing love and protection. I admired him and thought about how difficult it must be to have no arms, yet here he was, smiling and making the most of life with his son.

———

Before I became aware of how often depression and anxiety consumed my life, I simply assumed I was lazy. I was regularly tired, and I felt I never got enough sleep. I went through cycles of feeling physically weak and wondered if I was exaggerating, though I couldn't pinpoint what I was doing wrong. Those around me seemed to have endless energy while I felt frozen in my tracks. The fatigue limited what I could do every day, and I became massively embarrassed about it.

Once I started paying more attention to what my body did, however, I began to recognize the almost instant physical reactions my body had to my emotions. Since then, my body has become my greatest indicator. I've found that it faithfully warns me of any emotional dangers that may lie ahead. Rather than considering my body an embarrassment, I now see it as my protector. It speaks to me in ways that warn and defend. It points out threats and guides me to better places.

That helps because **for me to be emotionally and physically successful, I must allow myself to feel down while pushing to keep moving no matter how much or how little that is.**

The father in the library has been a powerful motivator for me. I'm certain he has suffered deep emotional pain from the loss of his arms. Yet, when I saw him with his child in the library, he was pushing forward. Despite his heavy challenges, he was searching for his yellow. See the charts below for the warnings my body gives me in response to my emotions.

Physical
Depression

Mild	I experience on and off tiredness. I'm able to have times of feeling refreshed and energetic. I may physically drop during or after certain experiences or at various times of the day.
Moderate	Fatigue is a constant battle. I feel my body dragging, and it seems as if it's pulled back and forth with my emotions. It becomes more difficult to get the day-to-day chores done.
Severe	I feel exhausted all the time. I often need to take time to rest throughout the day. I need moments of mental "zoning out" to counteract my negative thoughts. It takes great effort to focus on the basics of life.
Suicidal	As with severe depression, I feel exhausted all the time. It takes great effort to focus on just the basics. The push and pull is exhausting.
Numb	My days are filled with mental "zoning out." It takes great effort to focus on the basics; I may even neglect them. I may be exhausted or have heightened senses, but either way, I'm not able to focus or think clearly.

Physical
Anxiety

Mild	I start getting sweaty and have heightened senses. I become restless, and it's more difficult to concentrate. My heart beats faster than usual.
Moderate	I experience heart palpitations and muscle tension. It's hard to sit still. I have frequent headaches.
Severe	I am physically exhausted but mentally alert. I have diarrhea, nausea, and muscle tension. I cry much easier. Migraines may kick in. Shocks in various nerves and tingling in extremities may be present.
Panic Attack	I am consumed with fear and confusion. My body shakes, and I sob. I experience muscle tension, heart palpitations, nausea, and diarrhea. I have a hard time breathing. I want to be on the floor or in bed. I want to hide. I am exhausted.

(continued on next page)

Anxiety Fog My brain feels numb. I have a hard time hearing. I have difficulty thinking, focusing, and grasping concepts. I may seem clumsy or distracted.

Chapter 35

To Move or Not to Move

Exercise

I HAVE A love-hate relationship with exercise. Let's be real, though. It's more hate than love. I may go weeks, months, or even years without an "official" routine. I mean, I exercise here and there, but maintaining a routine is more difficult.

When I'm depressed, it feels as if there is a literal weight on my shoulders. It is difficult to get out of bed, much less exercise. It's a challenge to *get* moving. When I'm anxious, my heart races, and it is difficult to breathe. It's challenging to *keep* moving. But as I continue to fight for yellow, I try to keep a decent balance of exercise in my life. Sometimes it happens. Sometimes it doesn't.

If I want to get into a routine, I must be in a good enough place emotionally to do that. So even if I can't make a routine work, I look for things I enjoy that provide some exercise. Maybe it's going to the gym or walking with a friend. I watch for pockets where I can push myself. Sometimes it feels relatively easy, but most times, it feels as if I need the stars to align for it to happen.

If I want to push myself to exercise, I can't think too much about it. It may sound ridiculous, but while I put on my shoes, I try not to psych myself out. I create small, realistic goals and allow myself to relish in any progress I make. It can take weeks for me to not experience an emotional drop after exercising, which makes it that much more frustrating.

When I do get into an exercise routine, though, I get so excited! After getting in the groove, I feel physically and emotionally lifted. I can think more clearly and feel physically stronger throughout the day. One might think this lift would be motivation enough to stick with the routine, but, unfortunately, the emotional drop can strike at any point.

It's difficult to describe the demonic weight that pulls at and haunts the mind. People tell me, "Just push through it." "Just keep going.'" But when the emotional storm hits, I feel deflated. I get discouraged and disappointed with myself. All the progress I've fought so hard for is squashed. Not only is the routine broken, it gets put on pause until I can muddle through and find enough motivation to start again.

————

There are activities and exercises I do enjoy. For example, I like casual bike riding. My family loves this place in the mountains where there are fantastic bike trails tucked in the pine trees and the weather is usually just right.

Recently, I went biking with my husband in a small town we were visiting. It was the perfect weather and the perfect companionship. In fact, everything was perfect. But before you hear idyllic, breezy music, let me share how things went down.

I started to get anxious as we got the bikes ready. It had been awhile since I'd exercised, and I began to feel insecure, and this insecurity grew as I tried to remember how to use those stupid bike gears. It should have been easy, but with anxiety, my mind gets all jumbled. My husband had to remind me yet again how they worked. His explanations quickly became mush in my head. I felt more and more idiotic, and my panic blossomed.

Nevertheless, we launched into our well-planned, beautiful bike ride. We started going up and down small hills, but my panic continued to intensify. I had started a bout of panic, and whether I wanted it to or not, it increased as I rode. Here I was on this supposedly relaxing bike ride, and I was having a panic attack. It was embarrassing and discouraging.

Suddenly, I couldn't catch my breath, and we ended up turning around. When we got back to our hotel room, I felt deflated physically and emotionally. My husband held me as we waited for my panic to subside. I was frustrated with myself and didn't want him to miss out, so I encouraged him to go for a ride without me. While he rode, I continued to work on reducing my anxiety by reading and writing.

After his bike ride, I was doing better. At this point, I knew I needed to get moving and grooving. Otherwise, I could kick into a bout of depression from the guilt I felt for having ruined his day. We left our room and spent the evening enjoying the small town.

———

It seems that every time I try to do something active, I ruin it for those around me—and the biking incident was no exception. Luckily, or maybe unluckily depending on your point of view, my husband is somewhat accustomed to my inconsistencies. He encourages me but also knows when I simply can't do something. I was grateful that, this time, at least it was only the two of us, and since we were on vacation, we had a flexible schedule.

My anxiety isn't limited to bike rides. I've had bouts of panic while hiking, swimming, boating, playing soccer, running, playing tennis, bowling, blah, blah, blah . . . what seems like everything. Oh! Ice skating is the best. It *really* fuels the panic. You should see me on ice skates. Oh, wait. I've vowed to never ice skate again. Oh, well. Guess that's not something you'll have the pleasure of watching.

———

But I continue to try to exercise because I know it helps me clear the anxiety fog and sort through my emotions. However, it is really maddening when I finally get myself into a routine and a sudden drop knocks me physically and emotionally down. I never know when the drop will hit, and once it does, it can take me months to get back into a routine.

Even with the good things it does for me, exercising also seems to play with my emotions. I battle focusing on my body, and I tend to easily beat myself up. I get frustrated that I'm not in better shape, which brings on the need to fight body-hate issues.

Not surprisingly, this is a perfect window for deep depression to set in if I'm not careful. I must stay aware of my thought processes and not allow myself to think or believe anything I wouldn't think or believe about those I love. Every day, I have to choose to love myself and accept my trials and weaknesses, including those with my body.

I find that small, attainable goals allow me to feel accomplished. I can then accept the accomplishment for what it is. The more I own my trials and the limitations that come with them, the less inclined I am to beat myself up. And that, my friends, is a reward in and of itself. See the charts that follow to see if some of the reactions you might have regarding exercise during the various stages of depression and anxiety are the same as mine.

Exercise
Depression

Mild	I am sometimes able to exercise in order to fight sluggishness.
Moderate	I must take advantage of times when I am able to exercise. It becomes much more difficult to do anything physical.
Severe	I rarely have the "umph" to start exercising. It's a struggle getting out of bed, much less exercise.
Suicidal	As with severe depression, I rarely have the "umph" to exercise. It's a struggle getting out of bed, much less exercise.
Numb	I don't want to exercise and don't care that I don't want to.

Exercise
Anxiety

Mild	I am often able to motivate myself to exercise. Exercise can help balance the anxiety.
Moderate	Exercise can go either way. It can help with the anxiety or make it worse, which makes it difficult to decide whether to risk it or not.

(continued on next page)

Severe	It's extremely hard to exercise when my anxiety is this high. It's already difficult to breathe, and my heart is racing.
Panic Attack	Exercise does not cross my mind at this time.
Anxiety Fog	Exercise can help clear my mind a bit. Depending on how bad the fog is, I must be careful since it's difficult to focus even on simple things, such as walking on the treadmill.

Chapter 36

Just Don't Kill the Tree

Getting Out of Bed

MY BROTHER DANIEL was headed out of town and had just planted a new tree. It wasn't yet hooked up to a drip system, so he asked my husband and me to water it. Still, he was concerned that it would be dead by the time he got back. In addition to the blistering heat outside, he probably knew how skilled I was at killing plants. I'm a legend.

My husband and I faithfully watered the tree. There was no way we were gonna let him down. We were so concerned that we gave it extra water, just in case.

Oh, boy. Evidently, there's a science to plants. Go figure. Water them too little, you kill them. Water them too much, you kill them. You guessed it. We watered it too much and ended up killing his precious tree. Now that I think about it, I don't think we ever bought him a new tree. Oops. Sorry, bro!

Similar to watering a tree with just the right amount of water, it is essential for us to find a balance with ourselves. There have been days and even years when I have slept way too much or too little. Balancing sleep hasn't proved to be easy for me, as depression and anxiety can create severe fatigue and sleepless nights.

But the better I regulate my days, the better I seem to be able to manage my dreams and sleep. For example, I know certain shows and movies cause me to become anxious, so I avoid them. I find that my dreams are an indication of how I'm doing; I have panicky dreams or nightmares when I'm having anxiety and depressing dreams when I'm at a low. Obviously, I can't simply remove everything in my life that is depressing or stressful, but the more I pay attention to the things I am able to control, the better.

Still, each morning brings uncertainty. Once we add the natural physical repercussions of depression/anxiety to the daily swings of emotion, we've created our morning challenge. Will it be a dark weight pulling at us, begging us to burrow further under the sheets? Or might we awake with a startling abruptness that demands an immediate focus on slow breathing?

Awareness, having a purpose, and motivation play strong roles in how our mornings play out. Without these, we are in danger of experiencing a spiral rather than being able to balance our cycles. **Having a purpose for getting out of bed as well as something to look forward to each day can be the kick-start we need to get moving.** Creating simple, realistic goals can help us look forward to a day that could otherwise feel overwhelming.

Every morning, you have the opportunity to get up and do the best you can, to start over. You have the chance to begin again, searching for your very own surprise shade of yellow. Below are the feelings I experience with getting out of bed. Are there days when you feel the same?

Getting Out of Bed
Depression

Mild   I have negative thoughts before getting out of bed but am able to pull myself out and get the day going fairly easily.

Moderate It's easier to get out of bed when I am doing it for someone else, like my kids. I have lots of negative thoughts but try to pop out of bed before it gets too difficult.

Severe   It's difficult to get out of bed. I feel physically and emotionally heavy. There are times when I can't get out of bed.

Suicidal As with severe depression, it's difficult to get out of bed. I feel physically and emotionally drained. There are times when I can't get out of bed and don't see a reason to get up.

Numb   It's difficult to get out of bed. I feel physically and emotionally drained.

Getting Out of Bed
Anxiety

Mild   I may wake up suddenly and have a hard time going back to sleep. This works well when it's actually time to get up.

Moderate   I wake up suddenly, my mind racing. I may wake up in the middle of the night and be up for hours trying to fall back asleep.

Severe   I wake up suddenly, my mind racing. It becomes more likely to wake up in the middle of the night and be up for hours in a panic.

Panic Attack I wake up in sweats and have a hard time breathing. I don't usually fall back asleep for a while, if at all.

Anxiety Fog Waking up and kicking into anxiety fog feels like my mind is in a cloud and I can't pinpoint why. It makes it difficult to get out of bed.

Chapter 37

It's a "Catch-2"

Going to Sleep

You know how the nursery kids tell the nursery leader things about their mom on Mother's Day? Yup. That's fun and scary at the same time! Well, according to one of my children, napping is one of my favorite things to do. I guess it's not one of those things you can hide very well. With my kid announcing this to everyone, I felt very exposed. Just kidding. But really.

I obviously do love to sleep—especially when I am able to fall asleep. That's a bonus. After an especially exciting or nerve-racking day, I can forget about falling asleep until the wee hours. One of the problems with anxiety is that you'll wake up with a start and can't get back to sleep for a while. Meanwhile, you feel shaky because you're so exhausted.

My mother-in-law is one of the cutest people on the planet. She zips around with infinite energy and has an adorable knack for either making up her own words or mixing up what she's trying to say. I need to share this because feeling overly exhausted but not being able to sleep would normally be called a catch-22. Well, she calls it a "catch-2." I think she's on to something, and I've decided her cute mix-up is the perfect way to describe this situation. We may typically be caught in daily "catch-22" situations, but dealing with depression and anxiety adds a little twist and undesired excitement to experiences that may not normally be so difficult. To lighten the heavy experiences, I now call them my "catch-2" experiences.

See below for some of the ways I react at bedtime during the various stages of depression and anxiety.

Going to Sleep
Depression

Mild	I can usually fall asleep on my own, but it still takes effort and sometimes medication.
Moderate	I want to get away from the world, hide, and just sleep. I often sleep too much as I try to escape the darkness.
Severe	During the day, all I want to do is sleep and escape the darkness. At night, my mind fights sleep. I find myself engaging in mind-numbing activities to get myself to the point of exhaustion.
Suicidal	As with severe depression, during the day, all I want to do is sleep and escape the darkness. At night, my mind fights sleep. I find myself engaging in mind-numbing activities to get myself to the point of exhaustion.
Numb	During the day, all I want to do is sleep to escape the paralysis. At night, my mind fights going to sleep.

Going to Sleep
Anxiety

Mild   I toss and turn for an hour or two and have frequent unsettling dreams.

Moderate   It takes a couple of hours to fall asleep without medication. I have frequent, stressful dreams and may wake up throughout the night in a panic.

Severe   I have a really hard time falling asleep without sleep aids. I have multiple nightmares and often wake in a sweaty panic.

Panic Attack There's no way I'm falling asleep.

Anxiety Fog   My mind goes in circles as I try to wrap my brain around what I am feeling. I may welcome sleep as a way to escape.

Chapter 38

No, Thanks. I'll Pass.

Eating

THE OTHER DAY, I tasted three different kinds of sushi. You should be proud of me. Come on. How can someone actually crave fish that is practically still swimming? If I *do* happen to eat sushi, I typically stick to the tame ol' California roll. It seems pretty safe. Usually, though, I simply pass.

Evidently, I got on a kick and decided I should go on a little taste-testing wild streak. After some tasting, I decided there was one sushi roll I was going to forgo. I'm good with avoiding it the rest of my life. Another kind was okay. It didn't excite me, but it also didn't make me feel like I was eating rotten, raw chicken. The third was actually not too bad. I would have it again if it was placed in front of me and I was *really* hungry.

Surely food is a super close relative of our emotions. Eating can be a challenge when you're physically and emotionally needing to eat quickly, the food is not tasting good, and you have no motivation to eat. I don't necessarily pig out when I'm depressed, but I do know that my habits change. And depending on my emotions, it can be harder to fight nausea or cravings. What sounds good one day will make me sick the next. (That said, I'm not convinced my feelings about sushi will ever change, no matter my emotional state.)

Not eating triggers a drop in my emotions almost immediately. To keep my emotions in check, I must eat right away in the mornings as well as regularly throughout the day. To fix this problem, I've decided I need a personal chef. Not just any chef; I need an expert. The chef I am looking for must be able to provide fresh, delicious, healthy meals and snacks on a whim. In addition, this chef must be able to change the menu depending on my mood. Obviously, food must be instantly ready because hunger can hit me quickly. If I'm not in the mood to eat, the chef must keep the food fresh and ready for when I *do* get hungry. Is this so much to ask?

Oh, I have also decided that homemade, warm chocolate chip cookies are the devil wrapped in a clever disguise. Rude. Just rude. See the chart below for how my eating is affected during the various stages of depression and anxiety. Are you similar in any ways?

Eating
Depression

Mild	Cravings can be controlled fairly well. I can wait longer in the morning before having to eat breakfast. I may feel more comfortable with my body image.
Moderate	I may use food for comfort during uneasiness. I waffle in and out of controlling my appetite. I need to eat breakfast fairly quickly to prevent dropping or agitated emotions.
Severe	I eat out of comfort, then beat myself up. I eat out of being exhausted and needing energy. I must get out of bed and eat immediately to help stabilize emotions.
Suicidal	I often care less about what, when, or if I eat. At this point, I may have no appetite.
Numb	I waffle between a loss of appetite and not caring at all what I eat or when I eat it.

Eating
Anxiety

Mild	I can control my cravings fairly well but may have some munchies. Snacking on healthier foods appeals more to me now than at other times.
Moderate	Most of the time, my appetite is quite strong. I eat quite often throughout the day; otherwise, I physically crash.
Severe	Either hunger is strong and frequent or food makes me sick.
Panic Attack	Food is not something that crosses my mind or something I care about.
Anxiety Fog	I may find myself eating aimlessly or forgetting to eat.

Chapter 39

Looking from Another Angle

Fasting

FASTING IS A particular challenge for me. When I try to fast, it only takes until about 9:00 a.m. for me to feel the drop. Though I am doing okay physically, my emotions quickly start getting rocky. Though I do my best to fight them, I begin to hear negative thoughts. But I push myself to finish getting ready for the day and try to think positively. *I can do this,* I say over and over. *It's no big deal. It's all exaggerated in my mind.*

I've tried to convince myself that if I said my prayers and simply didn't think about food, I would be fine. But my mind and body have other plans. When I fast, my heart fills with anger and frustration, and instead of reaping the benefits of fasting, I lash out at my family. Despite my embarrassment at not being able to fast with the rest of my family, the darkness increases until I give up and eat.

The entire ordeal is devastating. I start believing the words in my mind, and I can't remember the feelings of goodness. I wonder if I have simply made up the feelings of peace, the Spirit, the yellow from fasting before.

During my fast, both my mind and my body collapse. Sleep overwhelms me, and I hope the bed will swallow me whole. I am unable to talk rationally or be kind. By noon, I am having suicidal thoughts. It would be better if I wasn't around. It would save those around me from my nonsensical bouts of depression and anxiety. The words. The thoughts. It's emotional torture. It's painful. I want to be done.

Over the years, I was confused as to why the downward spiral didn't stop immediately after I ate. But by the time I ate, depression had kicked in and wasn't going anywhere soon. It takes days and occasionally weeks to feel like myself again.

After years of fasting and struggling to stabilize my emotions, I decided something needed to change. This wasn't where I wanted to be, and I didn't think it was where God wanted me to be either.

Even as I write, I can feel the guilt rising from my choice not to fast. I want to be able to fast not only for my sake but for my kids' sake. I want to teach them about the power and strength it can give, teach them that God comes first in our lives and that sacrifices such as fasting are beautiful things.

Years ago, I was able to fast periodically without such a steep drop. During those years, I was blessed with opportunities to strengthen my testimony of fasting. They were humbling and allowed me to experience a deeper connection with Heavenly Father. Fasting can very quickly bring His Spirit close.

I am honestly jealous of those who can fast and enjoy the spiritual power it brings. But knowing that the Lord is full of mercy and love, it doesn't seem like He would want us to have such severe and dark drops in order to fast. Fasting becomes a different challenge for us than it does for others.

We must become creative. President Joseph F. Smith said,

> It can easily be seen . . . that it is more important to obtain the true spirit of love for God and man, . . . than it is to carry out the cold letter of the law. The Lord has instituted the fast on a reasonable and intelligent basis . . . but let it be remembered that the observance of the fast day by abstaining twenty-four hours from food and drink is not an absolute rule, it is no iron-clad law to us, but it is left with the people as a matter of conscience, to exercise wisdom and discretion. Many are subject to weakness, others are delicate in health . . . of such it should not be required to fast. . . . But those should fast who can."

There are many with physical restrictions that make fasting difficult and even dangerous. Surely President Smith's counsel also applies to those who have emotional challenges. Fasting, though naturally challenging, should be a powerful, spiritual lift and blessing. It should not bring dangerous patterns of thinking or send us into negative spirals.

When dealing with depression and anxiety, we must vigorously care for ourselves to prevent panic attacks or suicidal thoughts. The beauty is that the Lord knows what we can and can't do. He also knows when we have truly tried.

Since fasting has been so emotionally difficult for me, I have begun playing with the idea of fasting from something else—either a favorite food or an enjoyable activity I normally do during the day. We can fast from our phones, our music, or the shows we enjoy watching. I must admit that it feels like a cop-out. Maybe I should fast from something much more difficult—like not ordering from Amazon Prime for a week. Ha!

Another idea I am toying with is that instead of cutting something out, I could *increase* something, such as praying, journaling, or doing family history. Fast Sunday is a great opportunity to ponder our testimonies and think about the Lord's sacrifice.

One of the main points of fasting is to enhance our capacity to feel His Spirit. If we cannot fast the conventional way, we can look for other ways to fast. The Lord knows our hearts and recognizes the sacrifices we may choose to make. As I have tracked my reactions to fasting as shown in the charts below, I've come to know my limits and can adjust my sacrifice accordingly. Have you ever tracked yours?

Fasting
Depression

Mild	Fasting causes feelings of depression. It is as if my mind is spiraling at a fast speed.
Moderate	My body feels sluggish, and my thoughts become dark. It becomes difficult to get out of bed.
Severe	I am typically stuck in bed and want it to swallow me whole as I deal with my dark thoughts. Because of my negative thoughts, I lose the desire to eat.
Suicidal	Fasting increases suicidal thoughts, especially if they are already present. At this point, I typically don't want to eat ever again.
Numb	I either want to fast to starve myself as a punishment or refuse to fast and even binge on food.

Fasting
Anxiety

Mild Fasting builds anxiety quickly. I must carefully watch myself and decide whether to continue with my fast.

Moderate I get shaky and dizzy with intense nausea. Headaches/migraines kick in.

Severe Breathing becomes more difficult. My anxiety quickly kicks into suicidal thoughts.

Panic Attack I'm not thinking of eating. The thought of eating makes me feel nauseated.

Anxiety Fog Fasting makes it even harder to think straight.

Chapter 40

Is the Direct Line Open Today?

Prayer

IT WAS MY daily petition. I wanted another child so badly. Not only were my prayers not being answered, but it seemed as if the Lord had forgotten I existed. My desire to have another baby consumed my life.

We had been certified to adopt for a short while when the caseworker made a mistake. He had let some things slip during our phone call, which led to him prematurely telling us that a newborn awaited at a nearby hospital. Due to logistics, we were not allowed to go to the hospital for two days, at which time we would find out the gender of the baby.

We couldn't believe our lives could change so instantly! Running to the store, we purchased the needed newborn items, replacing those we had given to others since our first child's birth.

The next day, we received a call saying things had changed and we would not be receiving the baby. I was crushed. Though I hoped the little one was in a good, loving environment, I was consumed with grief. How I had hoped this would be the answer to my pleadings.

A couple of weeks later, I found out I was pregnant. The shock was numbing. I didn't dare get excited, afraid this pregnancy would end in another miscarriage. One morning while doing the dishes, I felt I should contact the adoption agency right away and inform them of my pregnancy. After I called, I went about my day and didn't think much more about it. That same evening, I received a call from a friend who volunteered for the agency. She congratulated me on my pregnancy and proceeded to tell me what had happened earlier that day.

A mother had brought her two-month-old baby girl to the agency; she was looking for a family to adopt her child and had selected our family. The young mother was then told I had called just fifteen minutes earlier to let them know I was pregnant. They were pulling our names off the list of potential adoptive parents, and they told the young mother she needed to select another family.

Oh, the irony! I was hurt to the core. I sobbed as I begged my friend to tell the agency we could raise this little girl. I was sure I would end up miscarrying again and lose the baby I was carrying. This little girl was our only hope. But we were too late. Another family had been selected and notified.

How could the Lord be so cruel? He knew of my deep sorrows and the depression that tagged along. We simply wanted to add to our little family. What was the point of allowing me to find out about two sweet babies, neither of which I would hold as my own? This must have been another one of His cruel jokes, I figured.

A month later, the same friend called. She informed me that the biological grandmother of the little girl had decided to raise her. So, after a month of being in the adoptive couple's home, she had been taken away from them. I cried again as my heart ached for this couple. They had held, loved, and cared for her and hoped she would be theirs. I'm sure their ultimate desire was the same as mine had been for this child—that this little girl was heading to a good, loving home. And even though that had apparently happened, I'm sure their feelings of loss and pain ran deep.

The Lord answers our prayers in ways we don't expect. I was angry I'd missed the opportunity to raise this little girl. But the Lord saw the bigger picture. He knew that within a month, the grandma would be raising her. He knew this would have been too much for my heart and could have affected my pregnancy.

It may seem strange, but I wish I could have thanked that selfless couple. I suffered less because of their sacrifice. My prayers changed with this new insight. Instead of pleading for my relief, I prayed that this selfless couple would be comforted and feel His love.

Seven months later, I was blessed to give birth to a beautiful, healthy baby girl. Even so, the agony of losing the adoption was still quite raw and humbling. Unexpected guilt rose as I held my newborn with an understanding that not everyone had such an opportunity. Through this experience, I vowed to depend more fully on the Lord and place more trust in His plan.

Prayer is a mighty tool that can open the windows of heaven. As we learn more about prayer and trusting in the Lord's timing, we can be strengthened spiritually and emotionally. Consistently praying is a sign that we put our trust in Him. It invites Him to be part of our decisions and lives. It shows He is our priority and that we are willing and ready to receive His blessings when He is ready to send them our way.

It is difficult to recognize answers to prayer when you're struggling emotionally. And feeling cut off from the guidance of the Spirit is so lonely. Experiencing this separation to the point where it is commonplace can instill doubt and fear. To combat this fear, we must press forward and purposefully search for yellow. We watch for signs of His love around us.

You may be especially frustrated if you feel you have not recognized His Spirit or received answers to your prayers. That's okay! You can begin by putting your faith to the test. Physically show Him your desire to receive answers by kneeling and pleading with Him. Notice that this also shows Satan that God is your priority. Tell Heavenly Father you are ready and waiting to feel Him near.

Continue to pray in your heart throughout the day. When thoughts or feelings come, pay attention. Watch for any positive, encouraging, and helpful thoughts that come to mind. Recognize answers that may come through other sources, such as inspired lessons, or conversations with friends.

Follow up by approaching the Lord yet again. Ask Him if feelings, thoughts, or answers are coming from Him. And then be patient. Continue to pray with confidence that, in due time, you will have the opportunity to hear His voice.

The charts below detail what prayer looks and feels like for me in the various stages of depression and anxiety.

Prayer
Depression

Mild	I am able to pray and often feel comforted. I enjoy the reprieve prayer can bring; it gives me strength.

(continued on next page)

Moderate	I plead with the Lord that I won't drop further. I look for a reprieve, sometimes a little more desperately.
Severe	Pleading with the Lord, I am filled with frustration. I doubt I will ever find peace again. I feel helpless.
Suicidal	I am either avoiding prayer altogether or telling the Lord I am done; I give up; I can't do it anymore.
Numb	At this point, prayer is purely mechanical. I feel no emotion.

Prayer
Anxiety

Mild	I pray often to feel relaxed. I am often able to feel comforted. I enjoy the reprieve prayer can bring. It gives me strength.
Moderate	I plead with the Lord that I don't spike further. I look for a reprieve a little more desperately. Feeling He is there is a bit more difficult.
Severe	I plead with the Lord and am filled with panic. I doubt I will ever find peace again. I feel helpless and alone.
Panic Attack	I am filled with intense fear and plead for relief, and I struggle to find peace during the episode.
Anxiety Fog	I continue to pray, though prayer feels more emotionless. Everything is jumbled in my brain, so I hope God knows what I am trying to say.

Chapter 41

Soak It Up

Reading Scriptures

FOR A WHILE, I stayed quiet about the fact that we were trying to have more children. I didn't really care if others knew; it was just painful to talk about. Experiencing two failed adoptions, a miscarriage, and multiple unsuccessful infertility treatments had been emotionally excruciating. Attending church was miserable; we were surrounded by large families and discussions about the importance of family. I often felt selfish since I knew I was already blessed with an incredible husband and daughter. Still, I couldn't push away the pain of feeling that more little spirits were pestering me to come to earth but I couldn't do anything about it.

As time passed and our struggle became obvious to others, I became more open. I shared my pain with those who asked. Surprisingly, I found it refreshing. The new support system I gained through being open and real brought me bits of comfort. It brought me yellow.

Letting others know about our desire to have more children also brought varying bits of advice from others. A lot of the advice was the same, and some was random. At one point, when our daughter was about five years old, we had been trying to have more children for years. I was at church talking with someone I didn't know very well. She suggested I read my scriptures more so the Lord would lift my depression and bless me with more children. Oh. Okay. Thank you very much for that.

I went home and felt horrible about myself and my spirituality. Was I so off track I couldn't feel the Spirit or receive answers to my prayers? Nevertheless, I was desperate to pull out of the rut of depression I had been in. I was willing to try anything.

I took this woman's well-intended advice and read my scriptures more. A lot more. The drop came quick. I pushed and read more, hoping and pleading the pain would go away, to no avail.

Within days, I had suicidal thoughts. It was devastating. There was a direct correlation between the advice given and my emotional state. How could life become so dark when I was simply trying to turn more toward the Lord? It was confusing.

Looking back, I recognize I was already severely depressed, my emotions fragile and declining. I reached out to the Lord and pled with Him, telling Him I was frustrated and trying but could feel no relief. I told Him it didn't seem fair; I confessed I was angry and hurt. Still, I felt no consolation. Had no answers.

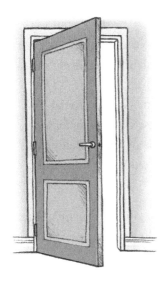

I was desperate to feel some sort of relief. I had to somehow get out of my destructive mind but felt stuck. Motivated by my deepest desires (see pg. 73), I gradually decided to explore what would happen if I did things I enjoyed while searching for yellow. I wanted to continue to do things that opened the door for opportunities to feel Him near. I wanted to allow for peace, comfort, and hope to appear.

When my emotions are dark, it is difficult to read the scriptures chapter by chapter without dropping deeper. So I look for various avenues to scripture reading. Rather than studying chapter by chapter, I may read a verse and ponder it, read by topic, or read Church magazines. If this still proves difficult, I look for other ways to invite the Spirit, such as providing service to others or saying more fervent prayers. **Being open to opportunities to *feel* His Spirit and willing to push myself to read again as soon as possible has been key.**

Despite not being able to read the scriptures as consistently as I'd like, I still want the power and peace they bring. I crave that peace and watch for it, experiencing it as often as I can. It was tricky at first, but I found the Lord blessed me as I trusted Him to help me.

In the April 2020 general conference, President Russell M. Nelson reiterated the importance of bringing the power of the scriptures into our lives:

As we seek to be disciples of Jesus Christ, our efforts to *hear Him* need to be ever more intentional. It takes conscious and consistent effort to fill our daily lives with His words, His teachings, His truths. . . .

Daily immersion in the word of God is crucial for spiritual survival, especially in these days of increasing upheaval. As we feast on the words of Christ daily, the words of Christ will tell us how to respond to difficulties we never thought we would face.

Scripture study is a crucial part of our spirituality. Surely this is especially true when we are dealing with depression and anxiety.

But what do we do when we get caught in an emotional drop as we read? In avoiding the scriptures, we create potential space between ourselves and the Spirit, which can become spiritually detrimental. This is a tricky scenario. We are again caught in a catch 2!

When struggling to read the scriptures isn't simply a matter of time management but of emotional turmoil, we can learn to appropriately adapt the commandment to our trial. We can push to keep the scriptures an important part of our lives by studying as much as possible within the limits of our emotional state. We must do our best to keep an emotional balance and not give up on ourselves or the Lord.

Watch for emotional windows of opportunity when it comes to reading the scriptures. When those windows open, study, pray, ponder, and immerse yourself in them. Soak up the experience, acknowledge the reprieve, and write notes in the margins or in a journal. Make notes of scriptures that give you hope and uplift you. Refer to them often. I draw hearts next to the scriptures that do these things for me. I also use labeled sticky tabs for favorite scriptures.

When I can, I read. As I read, I pay attention to the Spirit and make mental and physical notes of my experience. Soaking up spiritual experiences and replenishing what I can gives me moments to refer to when I am in a rut.

When the window closes and reading is not an option, we can still show the Lord we are physically and spiritually willing. When actually reading them is not possible, we can open and scan them, read our margin notes, or search a certain topic. We may skim them and spend extra time pondering what we have read. Some of the verses I love to ponder are:

Mosiah 7:33

"But if ye will turn to the Lord with full purpose of heart, and put your trust in him, and serve him with all diligence of mind, if ye do this, he will, according to his own will and pleasure, deliver you out of bondage."

This verse describes giving everything to the Lord: our trust, dedication, and our heart. He knows just how much we commit to Him and how much we hold back. It's refreshing to be reminded that if we focus on the Lord, we will be delivered out of bondage—emotional as well as physical—even if it's not immediate.

Mosiah 24:14

"And I will also ease the burdens which are put upon your shoulders, that even you cannot feel them upon your backs, even while you are in bondage; and this will I do

that ye may stand as a witness for me hereafter, and that
ye may know of a surety that I, the Lord God, do visit my
people in their afflictions."

It's tempting to wonder why we don't feel instant relief
or maybe even no relief at all. This scripture reminds us that
even though our burdens may not be taken away, the Lord will
strengthen us and help us through them. We must remember that the Lord helps us through various avenues, including
research, doctors, therapists, medications, etc.

D&C 24:8

"Be patient in afflictions, for thou shalt have many;
but endure them, for, lo, I am with thee, even unto the
end of thy days."

It's not always fun to have patience. As a matter of fact,
it's kind of a pain. It's not easy to wait for something we so
deeply need. Relief from emotional agony doesn't seem like an
unrighteous desire, so why can't we be blessed with relief? But
knowing that the Lord recognizes our heartache and will be
with us throughout our journey somehow makes it easier. We
will someday understand exactly why we had to go through
this specific struggle. Meanwhile, even though it seems like
He's not there, we can know we are never alone.

D&C 121:7–8

"My son, peace be unto thy soul; thine adversity and
thine afflictions shall be but a small moment. And then,
if thou endure it well, God shall exalt thee on high; thou
shalt triumph over all thy foes."

Here, the Lord is speaking to Joseph Smith and giving
him reassurance and peace as he's incarcerated in Liberty Jail.

Though his trials are extremely unique, this scripture can be related to all of us when in pain. The foes we triumph over can include depression and anxiety. Even though our struggles may feel never-ending, they are temporary. We will be blessed for enduring and continuing to invite the Lord into our lives.

———

When I can't open the scriptures, I pray. I talk to the Lord about what's going on and tell Him I am still committed. I then watch religiously for the next window when I will be able to read.

The scriptures can be a powerful way to feel His presence. We must not allow discouragement or the frustration of not being able to feel His Spirit affect our testimony of their power and truthfulness.

Tracking my responses to reading scriptures during my various stages of depression and anxiety has helped me to recognize when there is a window and I can immerse myself in the scriptures again. Maybe you've experienced feelings similar to those I've listed in the charts below.

Reading Scriptures

Depression

Mild	Reading scriptures can be soothing. I find it easy to feel the Spirit and enjoy the peace the scriptures can bring. My testimony of the power of the scriptures is strengthened.
Moderate	It is more difficult for me to read, but I can push through it. At times, I approach the scriptures with a "numb" heart—with little or no emotion tied to the reading—in order to avoid further emotional drops.

(continued on next page)

Severe	Reading exacerbates the depression. The severe lack of peace triggers feelings of unworthiness and self-doubt. It creates a suffocating sense of darkness and separation from Heavenly Father. At this point, I avoid reading.
Suicidal	As with severe depression, reading exacerbates the darkness. The severe lack of peace triggers feelings of unworthiness and self-doubt. It creates a suffocating sense of darkness and separation from Heavenly Father. At this point, I avoid reading.
Numb	I don't want to read and don't care that I don't want to read. I figure the Lord hates me and that I will get the punishment I deserve.

Reading Scriptures
Anxiety

Mild	I can usually read. Sometimes I feel stupid and need to stop, but I can usually feel the Spirit.
Moderate	I feel so stupid while reading. I can't think straight. I don't want to read but read anyway. I beat myself up for being so "unrighteous." Still, I periodically feel peace.
Severe	Peace is hardly felt. Reading is frustrating to the point that I often feel anger.
Panic Attack	Reading scriptures is not an option.
Anxiety Fog	Diving into the scriptures is difficult because I can't think straight enough to understand anything I'm reading. It becomes a trigger for feeling stupid. However, reading and pondering my favorite verses can bring relief.

Chapter 42

Out of the Box

Music

I CAN'T TELL you the names of music artists or songs. Just forget it. I won't remember. What I *can* tell you is that I love music. I love blaring it in the house and having dance parties with my kids, and I love to—ahem—turn it up kinda loud while I'm driving, like I'm twenty again. I love the feelings it evokes and the exhilaration it brings.

I used to feel guilty about not enjoying certain types of music, specifically particular hymns. But here's the deal. Some hymns just don't do it for me, and they quickly increase my depression. Trust me, singing certain church songs as you're dealing with suicidal thoughts? No *bueno*.

Check these out as examples of what I mean:

- "There is Sunshine in My Soul Today." Nope. No sunshine.

- "Have I Done Any Good?" Nope. I haven't. Just focusing on myself and trying to stay vertical, thank you very much. Chalk it up to another epic fail.
- "Welcome, Welcome, Sabbath Morning." Honestly, when I'm struggling, this song seems to mock me. I know that's not the purpose, but Sundays are already difficult, so to "welcome" another difficult Sunday seems, well, like it's mocking my pain.
- "Because I Have Been Given Much." Bring on the guilt. I've been given so much in my life, but I'm still not happy. What's wrong with me?

Don't misunderstand. Hymns are absolutely inspired, and we can invite a wonderful, powerful spirit when we sing them. But sometimes depression and anxiety result in a distinctly different experience when it comes to hymns. Instead of bringing comfort and peace, the verbiage can be painful.

For years, I assumed my battle with hymns was due to not being righteous enough or good enough. I thought maybe God was pulling away from me. I decided that maybe if I was a better human, I would be overcome with the Spirit and church music would affect me differently.

Not surprisingly, this wasn't a healthy or helpful way of thinking. It created tunnel vision when it came to finding the Spirit through music. Hymns don't exist to discourage or demean. They are for giving hope and peace. They are a tool to invite the Spirit. Music can heal our hearts and help us feel loved and remind us that the Lord knows us. It can help us feel His Spirit. As a matter of fact, when I'm struggling, "I Need Thee Every Hour" becomes very real and raw. "Be Still My Soul" instills hope and encouragement, for which I am truly grateful.

But if hymns are *not* bringing us peace or hope, it doesn't define our spirituality. Rather than writhing in guilt or assuming we are deprived of the power of music, we must appreciate that music is only *one* of Heavenly Father's spiritual conduits. We may not feel His Spirit through music at that precise moment, but this does not mean He has abandoned us.

As I continue my search for yellow, I look for music that speaks to me. The type of music that does this for me can vary depending on how I am doing. I watch for what brings the opportunity to feel the Spirit. I look for something different from what I listen to on other days of the week. I want to make Sunday special. At times, there is no music that brings peace or comfort and I prefer silence.

I still run across sacrament hymns that are difficult for me. Again, this typically depends on how I am doing, but feelings of depression triggered by a hymn can hit randomly. As I have learned that it's okay to struggle with hymns and that it does not mean the Lord has left me, it has become a bit easier to bear. I can plow through singing and use it as a time of proving to the Lord that I am here, ready and waiting for relief. I remind myself that music is intended to bring peace and comfort, but if I'm not feeling it, it doesn't make me any less loved or cared for by Him. See the charts that follow for the ways music can affect me while I'm feeling depressed or anxious. Can you relate to any of these?

Music
Depression

Mild	Various types of music can lift me, including church music. It can be a bit harder to feel a spiritual connection with music, but I am usually able to work through the struggle and feel His Spirit.

(continued on next page)

Moderate	"Power kicks" of loud music can help my emotions. I may not feel peace with church music; instead, it may make me feel numb. Singing at church is bearable, but listening to church music at home sometimes feels like a mockery of my emotions.
Severe	I am finicky about what music I listen to. It's difficult to listen to church music. Certain hymns create frustration and anger.
Suicidal	I become finicky about what music I listen to. Church music often increases my dark emotions.
Numb	It's usually impossible to please me with music, as nothing seems to settle me.

Music
Anxiety

Mild	I can listen to various types of music but may need periodic breaks of silence.
Moderate	"Power kicks" of loud music can help me relax. Church music sometimes agitates me.
Severe	"Power kicks" of loud music can help me relax. It becomes difficult to listen to or sing church music. It feels like a mockery of my emotions.
Panic Attack	Music seems to scoff at my pain.
Anxiety Fog	I typically enjoy a variety of music. Music is a helpful distraction from the fog.

Chapter 43

The Weekly Encounter

Attending Church

CHURCH HAS ENDED, and I'm back home. Though I am lying down, I'm still a little nauseated. My body feels heavy, and its weight seems to press into the bed. The air above me seems dense, pushing me farther into the bed. I curl into a fetal position and try to control the dark thoughts.

It was actually a lovely sacrament meeting. Though the songs were a bit difficult to get through, the rest was fine. The speakers were on point, and the Sunday School teacher taught in a way that was humble, tender, and kind. In the halls, I greeted those around me, grateful my secret about depression and anxiety had not yet been fully exposed. Still, it feels as if I am wearing a scarlet letter. I assume the letter is bold, obvious, and disgusting; I'm afraid of what my secret might bring upon me if fully revealed.

———

There is a contradiction between wanting others to understand so I don't feel alone versus needing to hide, heal, and regroup in order to survive. At times, it feels as if I am living a double life and that the joy others see in me is a lie. But deep in my heart, I know that's not true. I stay real to what I am feeling and take shelter at home as needed.

There are varying amounts of understanding, confusion, and respect when it comes to depression and anxiety depending on others' perspectives and personal experiences. When someone learns about my situation, I agonize over what they might think. I worry they will view me differently and treat me as if I'm crazy.

Brooding over what other people might think makes it that much more difficult to do things such as attend church. Opening up about my situation has been a scary thing, but with vulnerability has come strength. I receive support and love from friends who are genuine, and that has allowed me opportunities to find yellow.

———

Sunday mornings can make me feel robotic, but not in the sense that I have no choice or am forced to attend. As a matter of fact, it's quite different. The more I remind myself that I have agency and can decide whether or not to attend, the less pressure I feel. I choose to move forward, allowing myself to feel a sense of accomplishment as I get ready. I want to go as often as I can. Thinking about what I am about to do can psych me out and increase my depression and anxiety, just as it can with things such as grocery shopping or a school event.

I was surprised by how refreshing it was to attend church after we had been quarantined for months during COVID-19. I thought for sure I would crash. Though it was extremely tough to face social settings again, being with everyone was a loving, uniting experience, and my testimony of church attendance grew. Heavenly Father's plan of connection and support is a massive blessing and one we should take advantage of as often as possible.

Sometimes I still prefer—and even need—to hide from the world. I cross my fingers that no one knows I am suffering . . . unless they want to bring me cookies. *Then* they can know I'm suffering. Can you relate to any of the following feelings when attending church?

Attending Church
Depression

Mild	I am slightly anxious but look forward to feeling the Spirit and seeing people I care about.
Moderate	Attending church feels like a teeter-totter. It can be comfortable or quite uncomfortable. I am on guard and protecting my emotions a bit. I struggle with certain church topics, such as attending the temple, feeling the Spirit, or reading scriptures.
Severe	I frequently need to stay home. It is much more difficult to face others when I feel so emotionally dark.
Suicidal	As with severe depression, I frequently need to stay home. It is much more difficult to face others when I feel so emotionally dark.
Numb	I am quick to say hi to others but avoid conversation. I may feel frustrated, callous, or even annoyed by principles such as feeling the Holy Ghost.

Attending Church
Anxiety

Mild	I am apprehensive but fight through the feeling and focus on trying to feel the Spirit.
Moderate	I struggle at church. I can't focus. I have to try hard to smile at others so they don't think they have done something wrong. I can sometimes feel peace, but it's a gamble as to whether I will or not.
Severe	I struggle to get through all of church and may need to leave early. I can't focus. I rarely feel at peace.
Panic Attack	I am not physically able to attend church.
Anxiety Fog	I prefer to remove myself from people and conversations since it's difficult to think clearly. I can usually attend church but tend to keep to myself.

Chapter 44

The Goodness Does Not Change

Attending the Temple

YEARS AGO, MY husband and I were invited to some friends' home for dinner. These friends were the kind of people who make everyone feel like a million bucks. During dinner, the topic of the temple came up. As the husband was a temple worker, I immediately felt a bit anxious. I had not shared my experiences with the temple with many people. However, as the conversation continued that evening, I gradually felt more comfortable talking with him about my sorrow and battles with the temple.

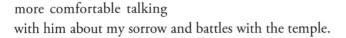

It's difficult to hear others talk about how the temple brings them so much peace. Granted, I have gone to the temple and have had some beautiful, peaceful experiences. I know *of* the peace others speak about, but it can be rare for me to feel that peace.

Determining your testimony of the temple—as well as other gospel principles—while in the midst of depression and anxiety is not suggested. Again, depression and anxiety cloud our minds and can often prevent us from recognizing or feeling His Spirit. This leads to frustration, doubt, and confusion.

When your depression and anxiety linger for long periods of time, consider going back to the basics of the gospel. Continue to provide opportunities to feel His Spirit again once the darkness lifts. Trusting that He will provide peace and answers when we are in an emotionally healthier state allows us the opportunity to let go of the worry of where our testimony currently stands. When we experience stagnant periods during our depression and anxiety, referring to past spiritual experiences as well as looking forward to future ones can carry us spiritually until we are able to feel Him near us again.

My struggles with the temple stem from deep insecurities. When I attend, I am confronting multiple triggers. I feel stupid, imperfect, unworthy, and exposed all at once. Depression and anxiety typically spiral at rapid speeds and, so far, it has been challenging for me to stay on top of those spirals. Attempts to visit the temple can lead to panic attacks in the parking lot or multiple days of depression afterward. In addition, I'm convinced that Satan jumps on this and wants to prevent me from having a positive experience or going at all.

Just because attending the temple is such a raw and emotional experience for me doesn't mean I expect others to have the same kind of experience, and I don't want others to avoid expressing their feelings about the temple. It's just that my experiences are different, and it can feel shameful to admit. And it hurts my heart. Oh, how I wish the temple was my go-to place of peace like it is for so many others.

Although attending the temple can be emotionally painful for me, I have a solid testimony of it. The times when I have felt peace are precious to me, and I am deeply grateful for them. I have had sweet and tender moments in the temple, which I treasure. The blessings of the initiatory and the quiet and calm of the celestial room have both consistently been my favorite aspects of being in the temple.

When attending the temple, it helps if I direct my focus to where I feel emotionally secure and connected. Places with more people around, such as the chapel or endowment room, can be a bit more difficult and bring on my social anxiety. Even if the celestial room is crowded, I can at least put my head down until it empties.

My experiences—good and bad—cannot be denied. I don't always have positive, peaceful experiences while inside, but I also don't always have bad ones. **The goodness and blessings of the temple are not determined by my depression or anxiety.** Recognizing that my "bad" experiences come from my challenges allows me to maintain a testimony of the blessings of the temple.

Though I may not attend the temple as often as I wish I could, I work on not feeling guilty and push myself to attend when I can. Attending when I am in a positive place has allowed me to have peaceful temple experiences. In addition, going with those who understand my inner battles gives me much-needed emotional strength and support.

I have routinely worked on recognizing and feeling the power of the temple and its ordinances. My testimony of the temple stays firm as I reference previous experiences and continue to draw close to the Lord. Because of this, Heavenly Father has repeatedly shown His hand in the work that takes place in that holy place. I am convinced that as I push myself to do what I can to keep my covenants, I will be blessed.

———

Only a few days after that dinner with our friends, I had the emotional and physical strength to attend the temple. During the endowment, my temple-worker friend appeared. We looked at each other as he helped me with the ordinance, and I felt a glimpse of yellow. It was a moment of understanding. The yellow told me God knew me, understood me, and had not forgotten me. He was proud of my efforts and understood my pain.

Charting my feelings about the temple has helped me know when I can and cannot attend.

Attending the Temple
Depression

Mild	It can be difficult to find peace, and it feels like I am "on guard." Depression can quickly increase, and I begin to carefully monitor myself.
Moderate	I assume everyone around me is feeling an uplifting peace that I am missing. I don't want to be there and feel as if all my flaws are exposed. On the other hand, I can also have some powerful, peaceful, truth-confirming experiences.
Severe	I typically don't make it inside the temple. If I do force myself to go, the experience can add to the low I am already feeling, and, rather than an emotional lift, I experience intensified darkness.

(continued on next page)

Suicidal As with severe depression, I typically don't make it inside the temple. If I do force myself to go, the experience can add to the low I am already feeling, and rather than an emotional lift, I experience intensified darkness.

Numb I have no desire to attend the temple. If I do attend, I typically become angry and feel worse about myself afterward.

Attending the Temple
Anxiety

Mild I can attend the temple, depending on the day and my level of anxiety. I can feel peace in between varying spurts of anxious feelings. My anxiety levels go up and down throughout different parts of the session.

Moderate It is very difficult to attend the temple. Anxiety kicks in and often becomes severe. A panic attack is possible if I'm not careful. It is difficult to feel peace, and I often feel angry. I typically feel anxiety throughout the session, even when feeling the Lord is there with me.

Severe I can't feel the presence of the Lord or any peace. I look as if I am full of fear. If I am already there, I may need to leave, but if I am headed there, it is likely I won't make it inside.

Panic Attack Attending the temple is not an option.

Anxiety Fog Going to the temple can quickly transition from fog to high anxiety. If I am already there, I will shut down emotionally and crash later, but if I am headed there, it is likely I won't make it inside.

Action

Taking Hold of What We Learn
and Moving Forward

Chapter 45

Don't Be Stubborn.
Be Stubborn.

Finding the Balance Between
Emotionally Pushing versus
Taking Emotional Breaks

PLAYING HIDE-AND-SEEK IN the woods behind our house
sometimes became quite challenging. One time we simply
could not find my brother Daniel. We searched for what
seemed like hours, to no avail. We finally gave up. He had won.

We started yelling for him to come out and immediately
heard his voice . . . above our
heads. Come to find out, he
had found a rope and
figured out a way to
shimmy up into a
tree. Mind you, the
trees in North Carolina
are not short, squatty
things. He was so high

we couldn't even see him until he climbed down a bit. He had intentionally hidden and refused to be found. Props, Daniel. Props.

How often do we hide in our trees and refuse to be seen? How often might we have support just a few feet away, yet we reject or deliberately ignore it? Pushing for our yellow requires us to *not* be stubborn.

Heavenly Father is our greatest support. He blesses us with valuable earthly assistance. Because the help we can receive from those around us is not only necessary and a *gift,* we must swallow our pride and ask for help. Doctors who will listen and allow us to openly communicate our needs are a gift. We must not ignore or be embarrassed about suicidal thoughts or feelings. Medication and therapy are gifts. Bishops and patriarchal blessings can guide and direct. Asking for blessings and praying like we've never prayed before can open doors to life-changing experiences.

There will be plenty of frustration. We are told we are given only what we can handle. But there's an important caveat to that: we are given only what we can handle . . . with the Lord by our side. Having Him by our side is a game-changer! The Lord multiplies what we are capable of handling on our own.

When I was growing up, we occasionally played trivia games. Oh, the death of me. Why don't we all sit around and identify each and every aspect of random knowledge no one should know? I think all trivia games should be banned from existence. Unfortunately, the torture my oh-so-cruel brothers inflicted on me in having to play such games has given me PTSD. Okay, okay. Truthfully, games cause me anxiety, but I guess I won't blame it on my brothers.

When I play any kind of game, my anxiety kicks into high gear, and it's frustrating and embarrassing. As my kids have grown to love games more and more, I have decided to push myself through the anxiety because I want to enjoy time with them.

So I have to determine where to draw the line. What are my limits? It may sound silly, but when my family wants to play a game, I mentally draw an assessment arc. I determine where I am on the scale of depression and anxiety. If I am too high, I decline the invite. But if not, I push myself to play.

This applies to multiple aspects of my life—not just board games. It applies to playing sports, attending church, going to the store, talking on the phone, exercising, having too much on my to-do list, certain social situations, feeling tired or hungry, being with people with whom I don't feel emotionally safe, getting sick, looking at social media, trying something new, and even certain movies. If I'm not careful, these can all push my depression and anxiety to unhealthy levels.

Obviously, I can't—and don't want to—avoid all of these aspects of my life. My being open and honest in my communication has helped others to know I am trying and that I want to push myself when I can. I try not to be ashamed, and I don't want to draw attention to myself or limit others' opportunities. But making this kind of effort is difficult and all-consuming.

Getting Heavenly Father involved in the process has been the most important key. It's been a great comfort to include Him in as many decisions as possible. He is aware of me and knows the desires of my heart. He knows my limits, and He helps me learn when to push myself and when to draw the line.

When we show Him we are willing to do as He asks, He will
guide us. In continually reaching out to Him, we begin to learn
our limits. He allows us to go through experiences that help us
grow and improve, places us in positions to serve, helps us find
yellow, and gives us the chance to share that yellow with others.

————————

A dear friend of mine, Candace, has been deaf since she was
young. She's one of those friends you might not see for years,
but when you're together again, it's as if no time was lost.

Candace was serving as a seminary teacher when COVID-
19 hit. Since she communicates through lip reading, masks
quickly became an issue. Rather than allow that to stop her,
though, she bought clear masks for her seminary students.

She always impresses me with how she handles her trial.
She is patient when she can't read others' lips, and she smiles
as she explains her situation to those she meets. Though it has
been extremely difficult for her, she never plays the victim. She
accepts the situation, allows herself to feel pain and frustration,
and then moves forward. She lives life to the fullest while blessing everyone around her. She exudes positivity and creates an
environment that allows others to enjoy the yellow of sound
while she pushes forward to find her own shade of yellow.

Pushing for yellow requires us to *be* stubborn! We can live a
positive, productive life despite depression and anxiety. As we
actively push ourselves and search for yellow, we will be able to
find it much sooner. On the occasions when we wait for yellow
to come to us, the journey is different. It's still possible to find
and feel yellow, but the wait is prolonged, and the yellow can
be harder to spot.

Frequently, I want to forget about searching for yellow or
fighting for relief altogether. The whole concept feels entirely

out of reach, and giving up on the search makes more sense than putting in more work. It's during these times that I must pause and make sure I am taking care of myself emotionally. Making treats for others and telling them how awesome they are takes the focus off me and provides me some desperately needed yellow.

Heavenly Father allows us to experience heavy trials. Whether we believe it or not, we are capable of fighting and discovering what helps us succeed. Keeping Him by our side allows us to keep our testimonies solid, even during times of torment. With Him, we can search for, find, experience, and relish in our yellow.

———

Flashes of yellow, so precious and quick, can be bittersweet. Pushing ourselves with determination can provide more frequent opportunities to feel and soak up the yellow. The glimpses will come. A moment here. A moment there. The more we search, the more yellow we will find. The more we find it, the more we will crave it.

So we must push ourselves and think about what we have done that has brought us closer to Christ. We can refer to physical or mental lists of the things that bring specks of yellow into our lives. We can try new things, give ourselves time to rejuvenate, read talks, listen to music, and talk with friends. We can create simple goals that can be accomplished throughout the day and relish the satisfaction of completing them. We can prioritize connecting with Christ and be loving and kind.

We each have our nightmares to deal with. The key is how we react to what we have been given. Elder Robert D. Hales said, "Suffering is universal; how we react to suffering is individual. Suffering can take us one of two ways. It can be a strengthening and purifying experience combined with faith, or it can be a destructive force in our lives if we do not have the faith in the Lord's atoning sacrifice."

I can't fathom having the challenge of being without arms. A friend of mine with a painful chronic disease once told me she couldn't fathom having depression and anxiety. The loss of a child or a parent, spousal abuse, chronic illness, job loss—the list goes on and on—there are so many very difficult trials, and none of it ever really makes much sense.

Here's the good thing: through the gift of agency, we get to choose how we respond to such trials. We can choose to do nothing by becoming numb or desensitized. We can allow anger to fester and grow until it damages us. We can blame God and question why He doesn't prevent the pain. Or we can ask the Lord to be near us. We can trust that He has a greater plan. In his April 2021 general conference address, President M. Russell Ballard said,

> *Waiting upon the Lord implies continued obedience and spiritual progress toward Him.* Waiting upon the Lord does not imply biding one's time. You should never feel like you are in a *waiting* room. Waiting upon the Lord implies action. . . . The personal growth one can achieve now while waiting upon the Lord and His promises is an invaluable, sacred element of His plan for each one of us.

For us to find the yellow we so deeply yearn for, we must act. We must do. Sitting in the same spot will find us, well . . . sitting in the same spot. Searching and learning bring us that much closer to finding yellow and feeling His Spirit. Searching for yellow means striving to find the Spirit in our lives no matter what stage of suffering we may be in. Awareness, acceptance, assessment, and action permit us to be illuminated with special, personal moments of yellow.

Chapter 46

The Recurrent Bloom

Through Him, We Can Thrive More Fully Than Ever Expected

WE NICKNAMED IT the "Sprite tree." No one we talked to had ever heard of such a thing.

The story began with two trees: one lemon and one lime. We are not natural horticulturists, but we thought the trees were maturing just fine. But then the lemon tree refused to grow any fruit. We figured we would simply give it more time.

After a sudden and unusual "Arizona freeze," the lime tree up and died. It was such a bummer. It looked as if the lemon tree had died, too, but we weren't positive. We figured we were gonna be completely out of citrus luck, but, as they say, "It ain't over till it's over."

Sure enough, the next summer, the lemon tree—which was six feet away from the dead lime tree—started producing tiny baby *limes*! To say we were shocked doesn't do it justice. We assumed we must have been confused and that it was actually the lemon tree that had died. Doubting ourselves, we continued to watch the single trunk little tree. To our surprise, it became lush and started producing juicy, healthy fruit.

We couldn't believe it. The once-barren lemon tree was suddenly not only bearing fruit, but it was producing lemons in the winter and limes in the summer! And thus its nickname, the "Sprite tree," was born.

The little tree quickly became our pride and joy. We got excited each season while we watched the now-healthy tree grow fruit. There was no special grafting on our part. All it got was water, sun, and periodic pruning. As the tree grew larger, it developed into something we could have never imagined.

We often feel we are like a fruitless little lemon tree. We are consumed with our ever-present depression/anxiety and assume we have no purpose. It feels as if we'll never amount to anything. *But we underestimate the knowledge and power of the Lord.*

Our Heavenly Father knows the big picture and has a clear understanding of why we must endure this particular trial. He knows what we are capable of. He knows our efforts, and He knows whether we are doing all we can. He is our Master and will provide help as we seek it.

The trial of depression and anxiety is one continual test of patience. Answers, comfort, and relief often come so slowly. As we care for our emotional selves and maintain our dedication to the Lord, we will evolve into something we never thought possible. Though the hellish trial may not disappear as we so deeply wish, we will be able to find bits of yellow in our daily lives. These bits of color will give us hope, encouragement, guidance, and purpose.

Our trials can become a source of learning and greater understanding. Searching for yellow means we continue to water our soil and stay in the sunlight, ready for the opportunity to blossom and grow. We will soon reap the rewards of the search, and we will find fruit we haven't noticed. We might even find fruit we didn't expect.

Chapter 47

In a Pickle

To Those Searching for Ways to Help

I OFTEN SIT and reflect on those who have helped, loved, and encouraged me over the years. The gratitude I feel toward you is real. Thank goodness you are in my life. It would be a bleak world without you.

Such is the case with every person who has helped, loved, and encouraged any soul who suffers from depression and anxiety. You are a blessing.

———

Based on the experiences I have been lucky enough to have with these extraordinary humans, let me share some insight on what you can do to be a spot of yellow in someone's life. When you see us, say hi. Hug us and tell us how much you love us. Look us in the eye and ask how we are doing, but don't mention our struggles every time. Simply offer a sympathetic ear, showing you want to understand. Remind us there is hope, even if we can't feel it. Ask how you can help. We may say there's nothing you can do, but the kindness of your offer will be tucked deep in our hearts.

Be open and kind in your communication. Ask genuine questions. Oftentimes, we don't mind talking about our depression and anxiety. We simply want to feel emotionally safe and accepted.

Feeling judged by those around us can be emotionally and spiritually draining. My Heavenly Father, Savior, and I are the only ones who know if I am truly striving to stay close to the Spirit. Suggestions of how I should improve my spirituality can greatly enhance the pain I already feel.

At the end of the day, how I am dealing with depression and anxiety becomes a game of trust. Others must trust I am doing all I can to move forward, and I must trust that God loves me and has not abandoned me.

In communicating with us, be sure that what you say is kind, truthful, and necessary. Communication should stem from a place of love and should be fully accurate and without manipulation. It also needs to be necessary. Unnecessary communication tends to be hurtful and often leads to problem-making rather than problem-solving. Keep what we share with you confident. Though we may be okay with multiple people knowing, let us share our story when we're ready and under circumstances of our choosing.

———

Don't try to read our minds or put words in our mouths; instead, if there's something you want to know, ask. Don't give us a list of quick fixes or tell us stories you've heard about someone being miraculously cured. Avoid telling us detailed stories about someone else's struggles. Don't get me wrong—there is strength in numbers, it can bring relief to know we are not alone, and hearing these things can bring us a sense of normalcy. It has the potential to strengthen and help us through the muck.

But, ironically, hearing about or seeing posts on others' stories, positive and negative, can add to the heaviness of our reality. We may begin comparing our perceived failures to their successes and start to wonder what is wrong with us. We might feel we are a disappointment since our story or experience is not the same. Be sensitive about how much you share about others' stories and when to share.

———

Everyone's take will be different, thus the predicament. We may have already tried the suggestions you want to offer, and it's discouraging to think nothing is working. Your recommendations could also simply be overwhelming to think about. Though suggestions are needed, listen first, then ask if we would like your thoughts or suggestions. Again, a listening, nonjudgmental ear is often what we need most.

When appropriate, consider offering ideas of things we can do together to relieve stress or distract us from our depression. Distractions from the pain or looking for our yellow can be a powerful tool, but keep in mind that searching for and finding yellow takes time and effort for everyone involved.

———

I find advice to be most tricky when it comes from someone who is completely baffled—or even seemingly annoyed—by depression and anxiety. It can feel patronizing as they share stories of someone they've heard about and try to advise me accordingly. The suggestions unintentionally become the "just do this and you can get over it" type of solution. If they are not able to show genuine concern and lack judgment while asking questions, I prefer they simply avoid the topic.

The "advice" I find most helpful comes from those who truly listen, who are authentically concerned about how I am doing, and who ask sincere questions. They ask what I am going through, what I have tried, and what has helped or not helped. Their genuine love and support strengthen me.

This kind of "advice" encourages my own questioning. I am prodded to sift through the stumbling blocks and challenging parts of my life. It stirs an awareness of any progress I may have made. I not only learn more about myself, I often feel a reprieve in the love shown by those around me. It naturally encourages my search for yellow.

———

We probably put those who are trying to help in quite a pickle. We want love and support but don't want attention. We want to know we aren't alone yet don't want to hear others' stories. We want ideas on how to improve but don't want to try new things. What can I say? We keep life exciting!

Tell us you care and remind us of the progress we have made. Watch for signs that we are pulling away. If we're not receiving professional help, encourage us to do so. We may get angry and defensive, but saying things that are kind, truthful, and necessary can bring us relief. Don't enable our behavior. Don't allow us to use our trials as an excuse for acting cruelly or inappropriately. Hold us accountable and love us along the way.

Having a safe go-to place is a must for each of us no matter our struggles. We must be able to share our deepest worries and fears. We need encouragement and reassurance. Being able to talk with someone who doesn't judge or treat us differently can be a catalyst for our healing process.

While we are in the middle of a panic attack, soothe and comfort us. Make sure we are in a physically and even emotionally safe place. Stay calm and allow us to work through the emotions. Give us reassurance and hope as you hold us in your arms. Help us not feel stupid or embarrassed. When the timing is right, discuss the panic attack and help us create a game plan.

When we are depressed, be patient because we won't believe a word you say. Despite this, we need to hear it. Allow us to talk and share openly, even if the words seem crazy. Help us become aware of our motivations. Without true and deep motivations, there will be no progress. Encourage us to create and use a "Searching for Yellow" list.

Use your killer patience skills; you're gonna need them. Remember that no bout with depression and anxiety is the same, and it can last for varying amounts of time. This is normal. Depression is miserable and can be miserably long. Ask if we are having suicidal thoughts or if we are planning suicide. If we are, get us immediate professional help. Panic attacks, though shorter than bouts of depression, are just as miserable. The fear and panic are real and severe. In both cases, death feels imminent, and we desperately need to feel—or at least recognize—that there is hope. Supportive and loving people can give us this hope.

———

Create boundaries that encourage emotional and physical safety for you. Do what's best for you. If it's too difficult for you to understand or deal with our depression and anxiety, that's okay. When you need to, step away. Do not care for us to the point it damages you.

Remember that at the end of the day, you can't change us. We are ultimately responsible for our actions as well as what we believe about ourselves and our situation. Love us, and encourage us to search for our yellow. Still, keep in mind that we are responsible for fighting for ourselves. We must be willing to accept the support you offer. Help us search for our yellow, but don't forget to search for yours.

To Those Searching for Ways to Help
Depression

Mild	I feel the sincerity of others and try to allow myself to believe it. Allowing myself to believe I am loved and cared for on the not-so-rough days helps me push through the rougher ones.
Moderate	I can feel love from others but experience an internal battle: I don't *want* to believe others' kind words (nor do I feel worthy of them), but I know I need to. I am still pretty willing to attempt hard things, especially when I have support.
Severe	I feel as if everything mocks me. I'm convinced others would rather not have to deal with me or my issues. I feel I am exhausting to everyone. I deeply want to believe kind words but feel like I can't.
Suicidal	I don't believe I have worth. I believe those around me are incredible and righteous and that I am holding them back from their potential. I look for reasons that I should not be alive as well as reasons why everyone would be better off without me.
Numb	I don't feel genuine love from anyone. I am too numb to care. Love from others feels fake. I am not easy to motivate at this point. I don't want to do anything others suggest.

To Those Searching for Ways to Help
Anxiety

Mild	Distractions can be a great way to help me relax.
Moderate	Testing various ways for me to feel yellow can bring much-needed relief. The search for yellow can feel daunting and frustrating.
Severe	Distractions seem useless but are desperately needed. Sometimes it's best if I remove myself to calm down. Doing service for others can take the focus off me and allow moments of yellow to shine through the anxiety.
Panic Attack	Being held by a loved one can be calming. It's horrifying to have others see me in this state but feeling hope and unconditional love is needed.

(continued on next page)

Anxiety Fog   Having others try to help or overexplain feeds into my feelings of stupidity. Others being patient as I have a hard time speaking helps me feel secure and loved.

The struggle is real. And it doesn't look like it's going to end anytime soon. What is it we need? We need to feel we can expose our truest selves and still be loved and accepted. Feeling that love is what gives us the strength to fight. That's it. *It's all about the love.*

Acknowledgments

PUTTING MY LIFE in writing has been terrifying. I could not have done it alone. Heavenly Father has guided me to dig deeper than I ever thought I could and placed the most beautiful people in my path. Words of encouragement have come while I shed tears. Texts have been received at times that proved they were more than just a coincidence. It's this unconditional love that has allowed me to divulge my innermost agonies and given me the courage to share.

Darren, you're my love. You're my support. I couldn't be luckier.

Alison, Natalie, Austin, and Kate—my babies who are practically grown up—you're my inspiration and motivation. You see me at my worst and love me anyway. I am awed by the incredible humans you are. Again and again, you answer my question, "Am I crazy for writing a book?" "No, Mom, you're not crazy." To which Austin jokingly responds, "Wait . . . what? You're writing a book?"

Candace Cottrell, you have been a blessing and inspiration to me for decades. You and Carl are two of the most genuine, Godlike people I know. How grateful I am that our paths crossed years ago. When I sent you the first draft of *Searching for Yellow,* it was a jumbled, hot mess of words full of raw emotion. You read that draft and saw me. You heard me. You loved me. You urged me to give more and gave me the emotional strength I needed to dive in headfirst.

Aly Clare, you are one of the strongest, most insightful people I know. You have a gift for taking the bull by its horns and have encouraged and pushed me to do the same. You have taught me to never underestimate the Lord, to go deep, and to think outside the box.

Kathy Aydelott, Kelsey Belo, Lisa Elg, and Bruce and Janet Holloway, each of you has rooted for this to come to fruition and become my cheerleader. Your unconditional love and support have lifted me and allowed me to push through my vulnerabilities. You always came through with desperately needed encouragement just when I needed it. I'm so grateful for your friendship and love.

My shrink, you have helped me over and over to keep moving when I am BO—burned out! You patiently smile as I say I don't wanna see you cause the last thing I wanna do is emotional work. You've learned of my deepest struggles and greatest joys. You've helped me to feel strong and lovable. You've helped me learn that pain from change, growth, and vulnerability is good pain. Lots of praying brought me to you, for which I will be eternally grateful. You know you're the bomb diggity!

Mom, asking what you wanted for your birthday or Christmas was annoying cause we knew we'd always get the same answer: "All I want is good kids!" Well, I think we all turned out okay. Hee, hee! In addition to wanting good kids, I think your long-term wish was for each of us to be able to fly. You wanted us to take what we learned and make the best of it with our own little families. Thanks to you, Mom, we're flying!

Rob, Daniel, Joe, and Jonathan Friend, even though you guys all got to keep the awesomesauce last name Friend, I guess I won't hold it against you. What a blessing to have four brothers who would at the drop of a hat pick up the phone if I called in the middle of the night. Growing up, you held my hand at the mall when I needed comfort, hugged me in the middle of the hallway at school, and helped me choose an outfit for those agonizingly important high school days, though I do remember a Barbie or two being blown up with the G.I. Joes—but I digress. You have been my advocates and carried me through hard. You were the men who taught me what my future could be.

Rob, Jonathan, and me in front of Grandmother's old shed. Daniel and Joe aren't very photogenic. Ha ha, just kidding. They couldn't be there that day. There is still no bridge over the small ditch to the entrance.

To the Reader

THANK YOU SO much for taking the time to read *Searching for Yellow*. I hope it has encouraged you and given you hope despite whatever darkness you may face. I would love for as many people as possible to find their yellow. If you've found this book helpful, please consider leaving a review wherever this book is available.

The journey to find yellow, though continual, can be a positive learning experience and one I truly hope you will consider experiencing for yourself. I encourage you to observe your own depression and/or anxiety patterns and see how they may or may not compare to mine. On my website, stephanieelg.com, free downloads and printables of blank depression and anxiety charts are provided to assist with your search for yellow.

To schedule speaking engagements, go to stephanieelg.com.

Best of luck in your journey,
Stephanie

About the Author

STEPHANIE FRIEND ELG was born and raised in the boonies of North Carolina. She received a degree in family life from Brigham Young University. She and her husband, Darren, have settled in Arizona with their four gorgeous children and three yummy grandchildren—a bit biased? No way. Stephanie is passionate in her faith as a member of The Church of Jesus Christ of Latter-day Saints. Her decades-long struggle with depression and anxiety has enhanced her love and empathy for others who walk this path. She has just recently begun to speak more openly about it. She is obsessed with reclaimed wood, chick flicks, crème brûlée, and building happy, safe places for those around her.

Made in the USA
Middletown, DE
19 April 2023

28884632R00146